EAT RIGHT SWIM FASTER

ABBY KNOX RD

◆ FriesenPress

Suite 300 - 990 Fort St
Victoria, BC, V8V 3K2
Canada

www.friesenpress.com

Copyright © 2017 by Abby Knox RD
First Edition — 2017

All rights reserved.

No part of this publication may be reproduced in any form, or by any means, electronic or mechanical, including photocopying, recording, or any information browsing, storage, or retrieval system, without permission in writing from FriesenPress.

ISBN
978-1-4602-9205-1 (Hardcover)
978-1-4602-9206-8 (Paperback)
978-1-4602-9207-5 (eBook)

1. SPORTS & RECREATION, SWIMMING & DIVING

Distributed to the trade by The Ingram Book Company

PREFACE

Hello, my name is Abby Knox. I am a registered dietitian and sports nutritionist, swim coach, athlete, mother of competitive swimmers, and wife. This combination (apart from the wife bit) has allowed me to see firsthand how nutrition affects my own athletic performance, the athletic performance of my children, also the performance of the swimmers I coach. Your body is like a high-performance car that needs the right fuel to perform at its best. By fuelling your body with the right nutrition, you will be able to train harder, recover quicker and give yourself an advantage over more talented swimmers with poor nutrition!

Nutrition is a complex subject. Add sports food advertisements, food fads, and celebrity-endorsed products into the mix and it is difficult to know what to do for the best. Unfortunately, you won't get a huge amount of help from sports nutrition books. Most are written as textbooks to help people like me (with a degree in, and a passion for nutrition) learn about the subject in great detail.

That is why I wrote this book. In essence, it is written for people like my husband (that's where the wife bit comes in). He is like most people when it comes to nutrition. He has no passion for the subject and he doesn't want to learn the detailed science behind it. But, he does want to know what to feed our children so that they can be healthy and perform at their best.

My journey to writing this book began when I was a teenager living in England. I loved sport (in particular, swimming and running) and I loved to win, so I was always looking for ways to improve my performance. I found that I was just as motivated as my competitors and I trained just as much, so I started looking for other ways to get an edge on them. For me, the obvious answer was nutrition.

In my youth, I competed nationally in both swimming and cross country running and at the age of eighteen, I won the British modern biathlon championships (swim and run). This gave me the opportunity to compete internationally for Great Britain and was one of the highlights of my athletic career. My interest in nutrition took me down the path to an honours bachelor's degree in human biological sciences at Loughborough University and then on to a postgraduate degree in nutrition and dietetics. At Loughborough University, I competed for the swim team and the athletics team and I soon realized that when I didn't eat right, my performance in training and competition suffered. Learning to eat right made a tremendous difference to my ability to sustain hard training and recover quickly between training sessions. I began to swim and run much faster and during my second year, I was selected for the 'British Universities' cross country running team and competed internationally – another highlight of my athletic career.

After graduating from university, my career in nutrition started with my first post in gastroenterology and nutritional support at Birmingham Heartlands Hospital. I worked there until I moved to the north of England for my husband's new job. This led to a new direction in my career and I worked in the specialist field of paediatrics and newborn intensive care at Saint Mary's Hospital in Manchester.

After starting a family, we moved to New Zealand to enjoy an outdoor lifestyle by the ocean. For a small country, it boasts a huge emphasis on sporting excellence. I resumed swimming with the Christchurch Masters' swim club and enjoyed competing again. With so many sporting opportunities and hard core athletes in New Zealand, I was drawn to a career in sports nutrition. After achieving an accredited postgraduate certificate in advanced sports nutrition from Otago University, I worked at the international sports centre in Christchurch which was originally built for the Commonwealth Games in 1974. I advised many athletes from a wide range of sports and really enjoyed helping them achieve their sporting goals through good nutrition.

With my three sons getting older, we moved again to Canada to live nearer family. My sons were now swimming competitively and I volunteered my sports nutrition services to their swim club.

While I was preparing for my first nutrition seminar at the club, my husband argued that most swimmers and their parents were like him and had little desire to learn about the details of nutrition. If the seminar was going to be of any benefit, he said, I should give the swimmers (and their parents) simple rules to follow: what to eat and when to eat it.

Following the seminars, I received many requests to produce documentation that swimmers could take home and use again and again. That was the starting point for this book.

All the information in this book supports the latest sports nutrition recommendations prepared by the nutrition working group of the International Olympic Committee and follows the sports nutrition guidelines from the national dietetic organizations of Canada, the UK, Australia, and the USA. There is no bias toward food products or companies, or the latest food fad. The book sticks to science-based nutrition with a foundation of healthy, real foods providing everything an athlete needs for maximum performance.

I have written this book for all competitive swimmers, from age-group through senior level to university swimmers, and beyond. I hope the information will help you to reach your potential and achieve your swimming goals!

Table of Contents

1. INTRODUCTION 1
2. NUTRITION BEFORE TRAINING 5
3. FLUIDS AND FUEL DURING TRAINING 11
4. NUTRITION AFTER TRAINING 19
5. EVERYDAY MEALS AND SNACKS FOR ATHLETES 25
6. COMPETITION NUTRITION 51
7. GAINING MUSCLE MASS 61
8. LOSING BODY FAT 77
9. IRON NEEDS OF ATHLETES 97
10. FREQUENTLY ASKED SPORTS NUTRITION QUESTIONS 103
11. EASY RECIPES FOR HEALTHY SNACKS 111
RESOURCES 119
ACKNOWLEDGEMENTS 129

1.
INTRODUCTION

To make the most of your training, it is important that your nutrition is right every day. You do this by:

- having the right pre-training snack;
- keeping yourself hydrated and fuelled during training;
- fuelling your body immediately after training with a recovery snack;
- eating the right foods for breakfast, lunch, dinner, and between-meal snacks.

To make an immediate impact on your performance during training, follow the advice in Chapters 2, 3, and 4 which cover pre-, during-, and post-training nutrition.

Chapter 5 is quite a long chapter that covers everyday meals and snacks. Your everyday nutrition provides an important foundation for your swimming performance and your health. Athletes who eat nutritious meals and snacks every day will enjoy better health, and longer, more successful athletic careers.

If you don't do the grocery shopping or cook the food in your house, you may need to talk to whoever does and ask them to prepare your meals differently. The most common challenge faced by age-group swimmers is that parents prepare meals to suit their own needs which may be too low in carbohydrates or calories. In Chapter 5, athletes will learn that they may need to consume more carbohydrates and calories than their parents (unless they are hard core athletes too).

Swim meets are generally long days with short bursts of intense competition, most likely at a pool that's a long way from home. Chapter 6 will give you all the information you need to ensure that you remain well fuelled throughout the swim meet and you can race at your best when it matters most.

If you want to change your body shape by either gaining muscle or losing fat, Chapters 7 and 8 provide you with the nutrition tools to do this. Remember that the best way to build muscle or lose body fat is to make the change slowly over time. Quick fixes tend to be just that, and people who lose a lot of weight quickly usually end up back where they started before too long.

I have included a full chapter on iron (Chapter 9) because of its importance in athletic performance. I worked with a medical doctor to review the blood test results of swimmers (aged 12 years and over) in my swim club and this resulted in many of them needing to take some form of iron supplementation.

In Chapter 10, I have answered the questions that I am regularly asked when I work with athletes and their families. There are a lot of misconceptions about different foods and their benefits for athletes, and these answers should help clear up a few.

The last chapter contains a few recipe ideas for pre- and post-training snacks. They have all been tried, tested, modified, and tested again on my family so I offer them up for your snacking needs with the utmost confidence.

You will see that each of the chapters has two sections: "the Basics" and "the Detail." If you want to make a quick start, read "the Basics;" if you want to know more, then "the Detail" is for you.

2.
NUTRITION BEFORE TRAINING

THE BASICS

A pre-training snack will prevent hunger and make you feel more alert, focused, and energized. You will perform better and enjoy your training more. As a coach, I can easily tell which of my swimmers haven't eaten a pre-training snack. They find it hard to concentrate and are less engaged during practice.

Choosing the right pre-training snack is essential to give you the energy you need while avoiding a stomach upset. Your pre-training snack should be mostly carbohydrate with a small amount of low-fat protein. The more time you have before practice, the more food you can eat and the more low-fat protein you can include. Here are some suggestions:

15 to 30 minutes before training	30 to 60 minutes before training	1 to 2 hours before training
Serving of any type of fruit—fresh, dried, or canned (a banana is a good choice)	Low-fat (2% or less) flavoured milk or fruit smoothie	Sandwich with chicken, ham, or cheese
Granola bar (less than 5 grams of fat per bar)	Low-fat yogurt (2% or less) mixed with whole-grain cereal and fruit	Baked potato with beans and shredded cheese
A handful of low-sugar, whole-grain cereal or crackers	Hot or cold cereal and low-fat milk	Minestrone soup and bread
1 slice of raisin bread or half a bagel	Toast/bagel/waffles with jam and nut butter	Toast with boiled or poached eggs

Always include a drink with your snack to ensure you arrive at practice hydrated. Suitable drinks are water, juice, and sports drinks (see Chapter 3 for more information on sports drinks).

BAD CHOICES for pre-training snacks include candy, high-protein bars, high-protein shakes, chips, pastries, pop, and energy drinks.

THE DETAIL

Many studies on athletes have shown that performance is significantly better when a snack is eaten prior to training compared to eating nothing.

Whether your practice is first thing in the morning or after school or work, it has probably been a while since your last meal and your blood sugar level will be low. A low blood sugar level will make it difficult for you to concentrate and decrease your coordination in the water.

The best way to prevent low blood sugar is to ensure that you have a snack before coming to the pool. This will help you feel more alert, focused, and energized and you will be able to train better.

Your pre-training snack should:

- contain carbohydrates for energy;
- be relatively low in fat and protein to minimize stomach upset;
- provide fluid to maintain hydration;
- consider how long you have before training starts (the longer you have, the more you can eat).

If you are travelling to an afternoon practice straight from school or work, you will need to pack your pre-training snack. It is therefore a good idea to have one or two snacks handy in your backpack so that you can eat as soon as possible after school or work has finished.

You should experiment to find out what snacks work best for you. The type and amount of food in your snack will depend on what foods you like, your individual digestion, and how much time you have before practice starts. You should monitor the effects of your food and drink choices on your performance in the pool and adjust based on your own experience.

Pre-training snacks for 15 to 30 minutes before training

You probably won't have much time to eat before an early morning practice or when you are rushing to the pool straight from school or work for an afternoon practice.

Early-morning practices cause the most difficulty because you don't have much time to wake up your appetite and then eat and digest something before you get in the pool. It is essential that you ate well the evening before so that you wake up with good muscle energy stores. However, you still need to eat something before your early-morning practice to help you feel more alert, focused and energized.

The following list will work well for you if you are rushing to the pool and only have a short time before practice begins.

- Serving of any type of fruit—a banana is a good choice.
- Low-fat granola bar (less than 5 grams of fat).
- A handful of low-sugar, whole-grain cereal
- A handful of whole-grain crackers.
- One slice of raisin bread or half a bagel

Remember to drink water or some sports drink with your snack.

Pre-training snacks for 30 to 60 minutes before training

If you have 30 to 60 minutes before practice starts, snacks containing carbohydrate (30 to 50g) with a small amount of protein (10g or less) and low in fat (5g or less) are usually well tolerated.

Good examples include:

- Low-fat* flavoured milk or fruit smoothie.
- Low-fat* yogurt mixed with whole-grain cereal and fruit.
- Hot or cold cereal and low-fat* milk and dried fruit.
- Toast or bagel with peanut butter (or any nut butter) and jam.
- Whole-grain crackers with reduced fat cheese.
- Granola bar and glass of low-fat* milk.

*Low fat is 2% fat or less

Early morning practice

If you struggle to eat anything first thing in the morning, you may find it easier to drink a liquid pre-training snack. Good examples are:

- Low fat* milk or low fat* flavoured milk (e.g., chocolate milk).
- Low fat* yogurt drink
- Low fat* fruit smoothie

  *Low fat is 2% fat or less

It is common for my sons to drink low fat chocolate milk before their early-morning practice. They find it easy to take in the early hours of the morning when they are still half asleep. They have it warm in the winter and cold in the summer, they enjoy the taste, and it sets them up to train well.

In fact, a recent study suggests that the carbohydrate and protein combination in milk may help to improve exercise performance, especially in athletes doing high-intensity interval training. So, consuming a low-fat-dairy food for a pre-training snack is a good choice.

If you suffer from lactose intolerance, try drinking lactose free cow's milk which is available in most grocery stores. Lactose free cow's milk provides the same carbohydrate and protein combination as in cow's milk so you will receive the same benefits. Remember to choose low fat milks (2% or less) as fat takes time to digest and can upset your stomach during training. It is best to allow at least 30 minutes to digest milk and dairy products before training.

Pre-training snacks for 1 to 2 hours before training

If you have between one and two hours before practice starts, there is more time to digest food. Therefore, you can eat more food and include more low fat protein. Good examples of low fat protein are eggs, reduced fat cheese, beans, lentils, chicken, and lean meat.

The meal or snack should provide plenty of carbohydrates (50 to 100g) and a moderate amount of protein (15 to 20g), and be moderately-low in fat (5 to 10g).

Examples include:

- Sandwich with ham, chicken, or cheese.
- Minestrone or lentil soup and bread.
- Baked potato with beans and reduced fat cheese or cottage cheese.
- Rice bowl with veggies and a small amount of lean meat.
- Toast with poached or boiled eggs

Poor choices for pre-training snacks

Avoid fatty meats (like sausage and burgers), oily fish (like sardines and salmon), and fried foods. Foods that are high in fat and protein will take your body at least four to six hours to digest them.

Other poor choices include candy, pop, sugary drinks, and energy drinks. Even though these foods and drinks give you an initial burst of energy, this is quickly followed by an energy crash (low blood-sugar level) that will leave you feeling tired and hungry with poor levels of concentration. Not what you or your coach wants!

High-protein bars and high protein drinks are poor choices for pre-training snacks. They are too high in protein and often very low in carbohydrate. These will increase the risk of indigestion and not provide enough carbohydrate to fuel your training.

3.
FLUIDS AND FUEL DURING TRAINING

THE BASICS

As you train mostly in water, you won't be aware how much you are sweating because your skin is already wet. It is important to replace lost sweat by drinking regularly during each practice. If you don't, and become dehydrated, you will feel unwell and your performance in the pool will suffer.

Having a drink as part of your pre-training snack is important so that you start training hydrated.

Make sure you take a water bottle to every practice and drink every ten to fifteen minutes during training.

What to Drink	When
Water	Up to one hour of training
Sports drinks	One to two-hours of training

Good sports drinks are Gatorade™ and Powerade™, but not the low-calorie type—you need the carbohydrates that the regular sports drinks provide. The powdered varieties of these sports drinks are useful when you must travel for swim meets, but make sure you mix them according to the directions (no less, no more) for best results.

Poor choices for fluids during training are fruit juice, fizzy pop, sugary drinks, vitamin waters, and energy drinks.

The **ONLY** drinks that should be in your bottle are **water or sports drinks**.

THE DETAIL

You sweat when you do high-intensity training, especially in a humid, indoor pool. However, you probably don't realize it because you are already wet, and this can lead to dehydration. Dehydration can contribute significantly to fatigue and be detrimental to your swimming performance. Both your physical and mental skills can be affected. Severe dehydration increases your risk of nausea, muscle cramps, and headaches.

Tips to prevent dehydration

- Start training well hydrated by having a drink with your pre-training snack.
- Place your water bottle within easy reach at the end of the lane and drink at regular intervals—every ten to fifteen minutes between sets or during rest periods.
- Start drinking fluids early during training—don't wait until you feel thirsty. A feeling of thirst means that your body is already dehydrated.
- Check your urine colour. If you are well hydrated, you will produce lots of pale, odourless yellow urine. But if you are dehydrated, you will produce only small amounts of dark yellow urine. (Note: if you are taking a multi-vitamin, your urine will appear more yellow.)

When sports drinks are better than water

Water is the ideal drink for practices that last up to one hour. For practices of this duration, all you need to drink is water.

For hard practices of more than one hour, consuming carbohydrates will allow you to train at a higher intensity for longer, compared to drinking water alone. During a hard practice, your muscle energy stores will only last for 60 to 90 minutes, so you will need to consume extra carbohydrates to maintain hard training.

Regularly drinking a sports drink throughout your practice will provide you with the right amount of carbohydrates, fluids, and electrolytes for optimum performance.

Recommendations for swimmers	
Water:	Up to one-hour of training
Sports drinks:	One to two hours of training

The right sports drink

The right sports drink will provide you with a performance benefit during hard training. The right sports drink provides an optimal concentration of sugars, water, and electrolytes (sodium and potassium) that are rapidly absorbed into your bloodstream. The sugars provide an important energy source for your muscles and the electrolytes are essential for muscle contraction.

Look at the 'Nutrition Facts' panel on the sports drink bottle and check that it contains the following:

Bottle Size	CARBOHYDRATES	SODIUM	POTASSIUM
500 ml	30 – 40 g	190 – 350 mg	40 – 100 mg
750 ml	45 – 60 g	285 – 525 mg	65 – 150 mg
1,000 ml	60 – 80 g	380 – 700 mg	80 – 200 mg

Drinks containing fewer carbohydrates than listed in the table will not provide enough fuel for your muscles during hard training of more than one hour. Conversely, drinks containing more carbohydrates than listed are too concentrated and will delay hydration.

Look at the 'Ingredients' list on the sports drink bottle and check for the following:

- More than one simple sugar e.g. sugar (sucrose) and glucose (dextrose) - this will improve the amount of carbohydrate that gets into your muscles;
- Natural flavours.
- No high-fructose corn syrup;
- No brominated vegetable oil;
- No artificial sweeteners such as acesulfame potassium, aspartame, saccharin, sorbitol, sucralose, xylitol;
- No added amino acids, oxygen, or herbal ingredients - studies show they do not provide any benefit;

Gatorade™ and Powerade™ sports drinks meet all the guidelines listed.

Low-calorie sports drinks

Low-calorie sports drinks contain very low amounts of carbohydrates and will not fuel your hard-working muscles. Low calorie sports drinks are more suitable for recreational athletes who don't require the extra fuel.

Powdered sports drinks

Some sports drinks are available in powdered form. They are generally cheaper and more convenient to travel with than ready-to-drink products. However, it is important to follow the manufacturer's directions when making up the drink to ensure that the carbohydrate and electrolyte concentrations are optimal for fluid balance and fuel delivery. Over-concentration will inhibit hydration and may also upset your stomach. Under-concentration will dilute the flavour, making it less desirable to drink, as well as making it a poor-performing sport drink.

The right amount of fluid

Every swimmer is different because everyone sweats at different rates. Some body types heat up quicker and sweat much more than others, so their fluid requirements are higher. Your sweat rate depends on your body type, how hard you train, and how warm the water and air temperature are. Women typically have lower sweat rates than men.

As everyone's sweat rate is different, all athletes have different fluid requirements. The only way to determine your personal fluid requirements is to carry out the following sweat test. Maybe you can convince your coach to help you do it.

SWEAT TEST

1. You will need to bring your weighing scales, towel, a water bottle, paper, and a pencil onto the pool deck with you. You will also need to work out the volume of fluid you consumed during your practice. An easy way to do this is to bring a measuring jug.

2. Before practice begins, measure and note how much fluid is in your water bottle. Then take a quick dip into the pool and towel dry yourself. Next, step onto the scales and make a note of your weight.

3. At the end of practice, towel dry yourself and step onto the scales again. Make a note of your weight and calculate any weight loss. Then measure how much fluid is in your water bottle and calculate how much you drank. Also, make a note of the duration of your practice and whether it was hard, moderate or easy.

4. Use the equation below to calculate your sweat rate and the amount of fluid you should be drinking during a practice.

Weight at start of practice minus weight at end of practice = body weight lost

Body weight lost (lbs) x 455 = **ml fluid lost from body**

(or body weight lost in kilograms x 1,000 = ml fluid lost from body)

ml fluid in water bottle at start of practice minus ml in water bottle at end of practice = **ml fluid consumed**

ml fluid lost from body plus ml fluid consumed = **sweat lost in ml**

Sweat lost in ml divided by length of practice in hours = **rate of sweat loss in ml/hr**

Once you know your rate of sweat loss per hour, you can easily calculate how much fluid you should be drinking for each of your practices by multiplying your rate of sweat loss by the duration of each practice.

EXAMPLE CASE STUDY

A swimmer weighed 140.0 lbs at the start of practice and 139.1 lbs after two hours of training. She started with one litre of sports drink and there was 680 ml left in her bottle at the end of practice.

Weight at start - weight at end = body weight lost

140.0 lbs - 390.1 lbs = 0.9 lbs of body weight lost

Body weight lost (lbs) x 455 = ml fluid lost from body

*0.9 lbs of body weight lost x 455 = **410 ml of fluid lost from body***

*ml fluids in bottle at start minus ml in bottle at end of practice = **ml fluid consumed***

1,000 ml minus 680 ml = **320 ml fluid consumed**

410 ml fluid lost from body plus 320 ml fluid consumed = **730 ml total sweat lost**

730 ml sweat lost divided by two hours = **365 ml per hour (rate of sweat loss)**

For a 1.5-hour practice, she needs to drink 365ml/hr x 1.5 = **548 ml fluid**

For a 2-hour practice, she needs to drink 365ml/hr x 2 = **730 ml fluid**

If your sweat rate is very high, it may be difficult for you to drink enough fluid during practice to match your sweat loss. It is essential that you start your practice well hydrated and continue to drink on a schedule of every ten to fifteen minutes throughout. It is also important for you to continue drinking after you have finished training to make up any fluid deficit.

Poor fluid choices for athletes

Poor choices are fruit juice, fruit drinks, soda pop, energy drinks, and lemonade. These drinks should NOT be in your water bottle because their carbohydrate concentrations are too high and their electrolytes are too low. These drinks will hydrate you slowly compared to sports drinks, likely cause a stomach upset and reduce your swimming performance.

There are many drinks marketed today as "sport" or "performance" drinks even though they are not true 'sports drinks'. For example, coconut water is touted as being the healthy fluid choice for sport. However, coconut water contains lower amounts of carbohydrates and electrolytes compared to a sports drink, and will not provide you with the same performance benefit during a hard practice.

4.
NUTRITION AFTER TRAINING

THE BASICS

Just because you have finished training, it doesn't mean that you can forget about nutrition. You need the right nutrition after training to help your body refuel, repair, and rehydrate. In fact, this happens best within the first two hours after training and especially during the first 30 minutes.

If you don't refuel, repair, and rehydrate after training, your body will literally start eating itself. In addition, you will be more prone to illness and you will miss your best opportunity to refuel and repair your muscles. Given that you will probably spend time in the hot tub, showering, getting dressed, chatting with friends, and travelling home, you will need to eat at the pool to get the maximum benefit from this 30-minute refuelling window.

Your recovery snack should contain:

- Carbohydrates to refill muscle energy stores: **REFUEL**
- Protein to repair and build muscle: **REPAIR**
- Liquid to replace lost fluids: **REHYDRATE**

Good recovery snacks

- Low-fat (2% or less) flavoured milk such as chocolate milk.
- Fruit smoothie (there are some recipes in Chapter 11).
- Fruit (banana) and low-fat Greek yogurt.
- Bagel with peanut butter and jam.
- Jam sandwich made with thick sliced bread plus a hard-boiled egg.

Even after you have eaten your recovery snack, it is important to eat your next meal within two hours to continue refuelling, repairing, and rehydrating your body.

THE DETAIL

Eating a snack after a hard practice is essential for your recovery and will positively affect your performance at your next practice.

The post-training snack is often referred to as the "recovery snack."

The right recovery snack will:

- replenish your muscle energy stores;
- repair and build your muscles;
- boost your immune system and reverse muscle breakdown.

To give you these benefits, your recovery snack should contain carbohydrates with some protein.

Carbohydrates to replenish energy stores

At the end of a hard practice, you will have used up most of your muscle energy stores. You need to consume carbohydrate as soon as possible so you can start replenishing your muscle energy stores. It can take your body 24 to 48 hours to fully replenish low muscle energy stores, so the sooner you start consuming carbohydrates, the more fuel you will have for your next practice.

Your body turns carbohydrates into muscle energy (glycogen) fastest during the first 30 minutes after training and continues to do it quickly (compared to other times) for up to two hours. This rapid glycogen refuelling is very important for quick recovery, which is why the first 30 minutes after training are so important.

This quick glycogen replenishment is especially beneficial if you only have a short recovery period between practices. For example, if you have two practices in the same day or an evening practice followed by an early morning practice the next day.

To hit the 30-minute window and maximize the re-fuelling process after training, you should eat before stretching or showering. If you wait longer than two hours before eating a recovery snack or meal, you risk having less muscle fuel for your next practice.

Combine carbohydrates with some protein to repair and build muscles

To repair and build muscles, your post-training snack must contain carbohydrates with some protein. We all know that protein builds muscles, however, carbohydrates are also needed to help your body transport the protein into your muscles quicker.

When your body digests food, it breaks down carbohydrates into glucose and protein into amino acids. When your body releases insulin to transport the glucose into your muscle cells, it also takes the amino acids with it.

Carbohydrates also boost your immune system and reverse muscle breakdown

Studies have shown that a low carbohydrate intake after hard training is associated with increased levels of stress hormones and poor immune function.

When your muscle energy stores and blood sugar (glucose) levels become low, your body starts to break down muscle to provide the energy that it is craving. Low energy levels cause your body to release stress hormones which depress your immune system and make you more prone to illness.

Eating a carbohydrate-rich snack with protein immediately after practice will reverse this muscle breakdown and boost your immune system.

The recovery snack: what to eat:

A recovery snack containing carbohydrates with some protein eaten as soon as possible after training is recommended.

If you are a smaller athlete (less than 100 pounds), you should aim to consume 25 to 50 grams of carbohydrates and 7 to 10 grams of protein in your recovery snack.

If you are a bigger athlete (more than 100 pounds), you should aim for 60 to 80 grams of carbohydrates and 10 to 20 grams of protein in your recovery snack.

Recovery Snack	Carbohydrate (grams)	Protein (grams)
Low-fat chocolate milk, 300ml	50	12
Low-fat chocolate milk, 500ml	80	20
Fruit smoothie, 500ml (see recipes in Chapter 11)	75	20
Large banana and ¾ cup low-fat fruit Greek yogurt	50	12
Bagel with one tablespoon each of peanut butter and jam	50	10
Jam sandwich and a hard-boiled egg	50	10

Immediately after hard training, refined carbohydrates such as white bread or bagels with jam or honey are better muscle refuelling foods than whole grain, high fibre carbohydrates. This is because refined carbohydrates are broken down into glucose much faster and will restore your muscle energy stores quicker. Fruit and sweetened low fat milk and dairy products are also digested quickly and make good choices for recovery snacks. Make sure your recovery snack is low in fat, as fat slows down the digestion of carbohydrates and delays muscle refuelling. You will also need to drink fluid with your snack to ensure that you fully rehydrate after practice. Include water, juice, low-fat (2% or less) milk, and sports drinks with your recovery snack.

You might find it challenging to eat soon after practice because hard training suppresses an athlete's appetite. If this sounds like you, choose the liquid recovery snack options such as low-fat flavoured milks, low-fat smoothies, and liquid meal supplements. Drinks are easier to take when your appetite is poor and are quick and convenient to consume on the pool deck before you go into the shower or hot tub.

Sports bars make a convenient, portable recovery snack. There are numerous sports bars available in supermarkets and health food stores, however, it is essential that you choose the right one. The wrong choice of sports bar will make it a bad recovery snack! Refer to the 'Nutrition Facts' panel on the package and look for a sports bar that contains:

- carbohydrates: 25 to 50g;
- protein: 10 to 20g;
- fat: 5 to 10g.

Remember that sports bars are not superior to real foods and they are expensive.

First meal after training

You should eat a meal within two hours of eating your recovery snack to continue refuelling and repairing your body. We will look at good meals in the next chapter.

5.
EVERYDAY MEALS AND SNACKS FOR ATHLETES

THE BASICS

Everyday meals and snacks provide an important foundation for athletic performance and health. Athletes who eat nutritious meals and snacks enjoy better health, and longer, more successful athletic careers.

Eat meals and snacks every two to three hours.
- Wholesome carbohydrate foods should make up half of each meal.
- Lean protein should make up a quarter of each meal.
- Vegetables, salad, and fruit should make up the remaining quarter of each meal.
- Eat healthy fats—cook meals with healthy oils and eat foods containing good fats.
- Eat nutritious snacks between meals.
- Drink plenty of fluids.

Breakfast of champions:

- Whole-grain breakfast cereal, fruit, and milk.
- Oatmeal cooked with milk and blueberries (or any fruit).
- Boiled egg with whole-grain toast and a glass of milk.
- Peanut butter on whole-grain toast and a glass of milk.
- Whole-grain pancakes (see Chapter 11 for recipe) with fruit.
- French toast (see Chapter 11 for recipe) with fruit.

Legend in your lunchbox

Use the table below to build your lunchbox. Remember half of your lunchbox should be carbohydrate foods, one quarter should be lean protein and the remaining quarter should be vegetables and fruits. Don't forget to include a drink.

CARBOHYDRATES	PROTEIN	VEGETABLES & FRUIT	DRINK
Whole-grain bread, wrap, bagel, or pita pocket Rice or pasta salad Whole-grain crackers Granola bar Oatmeal cookie Raisin bread Banana bread Healthy fruit muffin	Sandwich fillings: Ham, chicken, beef, cheese, tuna, or salmon Cheese string Hard-boiled egg Natural beef or turkey jerky Greek yogurt	Whole fruit (e.g., banana, apple, orange, peach) Bag of smaller fruits (e.g., strawberries or grapes) Dried fruit (e.g., raisins, apricots) Raw veggies (e.g., carrots, cucumber, bell peppers, sugar snap peas)	Water Milk 100% Fruit Juice

The athlete's dinner

Good dinner options:

- Spaghetti Bolognese made with lean ground beef, tomato-based sauce and extra vegetables (e.g., mushrooms or carrots).
- Noodles with stir fried vegetables, and lean beef, chicken or tofu
- Chicken breast (or any lean meat) with mashed potatoes and vegetables (e.g., broccoli, cauliflower, green beans) and gravy.
- Pasta with a low-fat cheese sauce and canned tuna or salmon and mixed vegetables.
- Rice bowl with chicken breast, tuna, or ham and mixed vegetables (e.g., corn, peas, and bell peppers).
- Chili made with lean ground beef or ground turkey, beans, salsa, served on a bed of rice.
- Deep-crust pizza with lean meat, chicken or tuna and vegetables.
- Large baked potato with lean beef chili, beans, or cheese plus a mixed-green salad.
- Baked salmon (or any fish) with boiled potatoes and steamed greens.

Snacks between meals

Quick and simple, nutritious snacks include:

- Fresh fruit or a fruit cup.
- Granola bar (see Chapter 11 for recipe).
- Greek yogurt, fruit yogurt.
- Fruit/oatmeal muffin (see Chapter 11 for recipe).
- Cheese and whole-grain crackers.
- Trail mix (see Chapter 11 for recipe).

THE DETAIL

Eating the right meals and snacks every day optimizes your training performance and promotes good health. This is a long chapter, but it will give you all the knowledge you need to make good choices.

All foods and drinks provide macronutrients (carbohydrates, protein and fat) and micronutrients (vitamins and minerals) in different amounts.

Carbohydrates, protein, and fat are all important, but must be eaten in the right amounts for best athletic performance. Vitamins and minerals are essential for good health and preventing disease.

As an athlete doing multiple hard practices every week, your balance of carbohydrates, protein, and fat must be different from a person who does no activity. It should also be different from your parents (unless they are also hard-core athletes!).

Let's start with looking at carbohydrates.

Carbohydrates: muscle fuel

Numerous studies show the benefit and importance of a high-carbohydrate diet for athletes, particularly high-intensity, aerobic athletes like swimmers. Simply put, carbohydrates provide your muscles with fuel. No other nutrient burns as efficiently as carbohydrates do. The International Olympic Committee nutrition working group emphasize that athletes must consume enough carbohydrates everyday to fuel their training program and optimize their recovery after workouts.

When you eat carbohydrate, your body breaks it down into glucose and provides energy to every hard-working cell in your body. Your body also stores extra carbohydrate in your muscles as glycogen which you use as an energy reservoir during hard training.

Without enough carbohydrates in your diet, your swimming performance will suffer. You will feel tired and you won't have the same desire to train hard. Without enough carbohydrates in your diet, you will literally feel like you are swimming through mud. That happened to me on several occasions at University, before I knew better, and those training sessions were a complete waste of time!

To maximize your training performance, it is essential to start each practice with full muscle glycogen stores. To do this, you need to eat plenty of carbohydrate every day to refill your depleted glycogen stores. After a long, hard practice, it can take 24 to 48 hours to fully replenish very low glycogen stores. Therefore, every meal and snack (not just your pre- and post-training snacks) must be based on a carbohydrate food.

You have probably heard carbohydrates described in different ways. Carbohydrates that are good for your health are often referred to as "good carbs". On the other hand, carbohydrates that are not so good for your health are referred to as "refined carbs". Let's look at both categories and when you should be eating them.

Good carbs

Examples include:

- Whole grains:
    - Whole wheat
    - Brown or wild rice
    - Oats
    - Quinoa
    - Whole rye
    - Whole barley
- Whole-grain breads, wraps, bagels
- Whole-grain breakfast cereals
- Oatmeal
- Whole-grain pasta
- Fruits - all types
- Starchy veggies:
    - Potatoes
    - Sweet potatoes
    - Yams
    - Squashes
    - Pumpkin
    - Corn
    - Carrots
- Legumes:
    - Beans (all types)
    - Peas
    - Lentils
    - Chick peas

- Other grains: Millet
  Amaranth
  Buckwheat
  Sorghum

It is important that most of your meals and snacks are based on these good carbs. Most good carbs provide you with longer-lasting energy. They also provide your body with the vitamins, minerals, and fibre that are essential for good health.

To check that products like breads, breakfast cereals, and pastas are truly whole grain, it is important to read the ingredients list. The first ingredient should be "whole grain"—for example, "whole wheat" or "whole-grain wheat." Be aware of the marketing words on packaging. Look for terms like "100% whole grain," but be careful of terms like "multi-grain" and "made with whole grains," as the product is not likely to be 100% whole grain. Always check the ingredients list to be sure.

Refined carbs

Examples include:

- Products made from white flour:
  white bread, buns, wraps, bagels,
  muffins, cakes, cookies,
  crackers, pretzels
  white pasta, noodles
- Potato chips, crisps, processed snack foods
- High sugar, low fibre breakfast cereals
- Sugary drinks, soda pop, energy drinks
- Sports drinks
- Fruit juice
- Honey, jams, syrups, sugar
- Sweets and candy

Most refined carbs provide you with short lasting energy and contain little or no nutrition. They should only be consumed occasionally as part of your healthy diet.

During and directly after training

Athletes benefit from consuming refined carbs during and directly after training.

During training, refined carbs in sports drinks are digested very quickly and provide quick, easy to burn fuel for your hard-working muscles.

Directly after training, refined carbohydrates restore your depleted muscle energy stores faster than most good carbs. Therefore, including some refined carbs in your recovery snack will help to speed up your recovery after a hard practice.

Protein foods—muscle repairer

Protein is well known for its role in building and repairing muscles. It is also needed for normal growth and development, especially important if you're a teen athlete who is growing and maturing.

Good sources of protein include beef, lamb, pork, chicken, turkey, fish, legumes (chick peas, beans, and lentils), eggs. Other good sources of protein include milk, yogurt, cheese, and soy products.

How much protein?

You have higher protein needs than a non-athlete, however, it is not necessary eat huge amounts of protein or supplement with protein powder. You can easily get all the protein you need from your regular meals and snacks.

If you want to build muscle mass, you have the highest protein need —but, this is not as high as you might think. Please refer to Chapter 7, "Gaining Weight and Muscle Mass," if this applies to you.

Most of you will easily meet your protein needs by eating one to two servings of meat or chicken or fish plus two to three servings of dairy foods (especially milk and yogurt) each day. Remember, the amount of protein you need at each meal is about the size and thickness of the palm of your hand. For most people, this is about a 3 or 4 oz. (90 to 120-gram) serving of meat.

If you eat a plant based diet, it is essential to include a wide variety of plant-based protein foods every day. Good food sources of plant based protein are quinoa, buckwheat, amaranth, Eziekel bread, soy beans, soy products, lentils, chickpeas, hemp seeds and chia seeds. However, plant based protein foods are not complete proteins, so you must combine different plant based protein foods at every meal to ensure your body receives all the protein it needs.

Be aware that almond milk, rice milk, and hemp milk contain little protein. Many people mistakenly believe that almond milk contains lots of protein because almonds are a good source of protein. However, when almond milk is made, the almond pulp (which contains the protein) is strained from the liquid, resulting in milk that is very low in protein.

If you are concerned about your protein intake, consider working with a registered dietitian who can assess your diet and advise you accordingly.

ONE SERVING of protein is:

- 3-4 oz. (90-120 g) cooked meat, poultry, or fish
- ¾ cup ground beef, chicken, or turkey
- 1 cup legumes (beans, lentils, chick peas)
- 1 cup tofu
- 1 cup (240 ml) cow or soy milk
- ¾ cup (175 g) Greek yogurt
- 2 oz. (60 g) cheese
- 2 eggs

Milk and dairy foods: builds bone and repairs muscle

In addition to being a good source of protein, milk and dairy foods provide a great source of calcium to build strong, dense bones and teeth. If you are a child or teen, you should have three to four servings of milk and dairy foods every day. If you are an adult athlete, you should have two to three servings of milk and dairy foods every day.

One serving is   1 cup (240 ml) milk
                  ¾ cup (175 ml) yogurt
                  1½ oz. (40 g) cheese

If you avoid milk and dairy foods, your dietary sources of calcium include leafy green vegetables, fish with edible bones (for example, salmon and sardines), nuts, seeds and fortified alternative milk products.

Alternative milk products made from soy, rice, almonds, or hemp and are not naturally high in calcium. Make sure that you read the nutritional label to check that it has been fortified with calcium. Always shake the contents of the carton well before drinking, as the added calcium tends to settle at the bottom.

If you don't consume fortified alternative milk products, you will need to take a daily calcium supplement.

Vegetables and fruits: protects health

Fruits and vegetables contain micronutrients that protect you against many diseases including cancer, heart disease, and eye disease. The different colours of fruits and vegetables provide you with different health benefits, so you (and everybody in your family) should indulge in a variety of different coloured fruits and vegetables everyday. You should include two servings (one cup) of vegetables or salad with every meal and eat fruits for your snacks and desserts. This will help you reach the recommended target of three to five servings of vegetables and two to four servings of fruit each day.

One serving is:

- one whole fruit
- ½ cup smaller fruits
- ½ cup cooked vegetables
- ½ cup of salad greens
- ½ cup 100% fruit or vegetable juice

Try the following tips to increase your daily intake of vegetables and fruits:

- Add extra vegetables such as corn, peas, or mushrooms to the sauce of your pasta meals.
- Add frozen vegetables to stews or stir fries for a quick, easy addition to your evening meal. Frozen vegetables contain just as many nutrients (or even more) than fresh vegetables.
- Add extra cans of tomato sauce or chopped tomatoes to sauce-based meals such chili, Bolognese, curry.
- Canned fruits in 100% juice make a quick, easy dessert with yogurt or ice cream
- 100% fruit and vegetable juices provide quick, convenient nutrition. Include a 100% juice or vegetable box in your lunchbox.
- Pre-washed mixed salad greens are convenient and more nutritious than eating one type of salad green. Add chopped-up fruit (strawberries, apple, kiwi fruit), shredded vegetables (carrot, cabbage), or dried fruit (raisins or cranberries) to make your salad more interesting.
- Add a handful of leafy greens such as spinach or kale to a homemade smoothie. I promise you won't taste them! A smoothie makes a quick, easy breakfast and is great pre- or post-training snack (see Chapter 11 for smoothie recipe ideas).
- Dried fruits are convenient and portable. Small packs of dried fruit are ideal for your lunchbox.

Most of your servings should be whole fruits and vegetables in preference to juice. Whole fruits and vegetables contain fibre which is essential for your health, particularly your heart and digestive system.

Fats: the good and the bad

There are two broad categories of good fats: monounsaturated and polyunsaturated fats.

A big study in the 1960s revealed that people in Greece and other parts of the Mediterranean region had a low rate of heart disease despite their high-fat diet. The main fat in their diet was olive oil, which contains mainly monounsaturated fat. Other good sources of monounsaturated fat (MUFAs) are peanut oil, canola oil, avocados, olives and most nuts.

Polyunsaturated fats are required for normal body functions—but your body can't make them, so you must get them from your food. There are two main types of polyunsaturated fats: omega-3 and omega-6. Most people get enough omega-6 fats in their usual diet but typically fall short on omega-3 fats.

Good food sources of omega-3 fats include oily fish (e.g., salmon, mackerel, and sardines), ground flaxseed, chia seeds, and walnuts. Omega-3 fats are essential for normal brain function and preventing heart disease and stroke. Research also suggests that omega-3 fats help athletes recover quicker by reducing exercise-related inflammation and muscle soreness.

You should eat all types of "good fats" every day:

- Extra virgin olive oil and flaxseed oil are great for salad dressings, dipping and drizzling.
- Canola oil, avocado oil and coconut oil are great for sautéing, stir fries, and high-heat cooking.
- Nuts, such as walnuts, almonds, cashews, pecans and peanuts—try making a tasty trail mix snack by adding some dried fruits (see recipe in Chapter 11).
- Nut butters, such as peanut butter, almond butter, and cashew butter. Choose 100% nut butters with no added salt or sugar.
- Seeds, such as sunflower, pumpkin, sesame, flax, chia, and hemp are good for sprinkling on salads or adding to your breakfast cereal.
- Avocados are delicious chopped up in salads or spread on bread instead of butter.
- Oily fish, such as wild salmon, sardines and mackerel—aim for two servings of oily fish each week.

Bad fats

Trans fats are the worst type of dietary fat. They are produced when a vegetable oil is turned into a solid fat to extend a food's shelf life. Trans fats create inflammation and increase the risk of cancer, heart disease, stroke, and diabetes.

Trans fats are found in processed foods such as cookies, cakes, crackers, pastries, and microwave popcorn. Since 2006, food manufacturers have been required to list trans-fat content on food labels. Consequently, the food industry has reduced trans fats in many foods. Always check the ingredient list. If you see the words, "hydrogenated oil" or "partially hydrogenated oil," the product has trans fat in it and you should avoid it.

Saturated fats are common in the Western diet and are found in meat, whole milk and whole dairy products (cheese, butter, cream, sour cream, full-fat yogurt). In recent years, studies indicate that saturated fats may not be as harmful as once thought, however, it is still advisable to limit your intake of saturated fat until we know more. Choose lean cuts of meat, remove any visible white fats before eating and enjoy cream and butter in moderation.

Meals

Now that you understand the importance of carbohydrates, proteins, and fats, let's use that knowledge to build the best meals for athletes.

Breakfast of champions

Your breakfast is one of the most important meals of the day and you should never skip it. Breakfast literally means "break your fast," because you have not eaten for many hours while you've been sleeping. Eating breakfast within half an hour of waking will increase your energy levels and help you concentrate for your morning ahead at school or work. It is also an opportunity to increase your muscle energy stores for your next training session.

Good breakfast choices

- Whole-grain breakfast cereal and milk
- Oatmeal cooked with milk and blueberries (or any fruit).
- Boiled egg with whole-grain toast and glass of milk.
- Peanut butter (or any nut butter) on whole-grain toast and a glass of milk.
- Whole-grain pancakes (see Chapter 11 for recipe) with fruit.
- French toast (see Chapter 11 for recipe) with fruit.

Remember, if you have an early-morning practice, you will not have enough time to digest a full breakfast, so you should have a pre-training snack (Chapter 2) and then eat your breakfast soon after your practice has finished.

Choosing a good breakfast cereal

There are so many different choices of breakfast cereal that it can be difficult to distinguish the good ones from those that are more like boxes of candy.

To choose a good breakfast cereal, look closely at the 'Nutrition Facts' panel and the 'Ingredients' list:

Nutrition Facts Panel	Ingredients List
8g or less of sugar per serving	Whole-grains are listed first
3g or more of fibre per serving	Few ingredients
4g or more of protein per serving	No hydrogenated or partially hydrogenated oils
0g Trans Fat	No artificial colours, artificial flavours and ingredients that you can't pronounce!

A legend in your lunchbox

You probably take a lunchbox to school or work—it is essential to pack it with the right foods and fluids to make a healthy lunch. Listed below are lunchbox foods that provide carbohydrates, proteins, vegetables and fruit.

Remember, half of your lunchbox should be wholesome carbohydrate foods ("good carbs"), one quarter should be protein-rich foods, and the remaining quarter should be vegetables and fruit.

Don't forget to pack a water bottle with your lunchbox. Milk and 100% juice boxes are also good choices of fluids.

Select something from each of the headings below and become a legend in your lunchbox.

CARBOHYDRATES	PROTEIN	VEGETABLES & FRUIT	DRINK
Whole-grain bread, wrap, bagel, or pita pocket Rice or pasta salad Whole-grain crackers Granola bar Oatmeal cookie Raisin bread Banana bread Healthy fruit muffin	Sandwich fillings: ham, chicken, turkey, beef, cheese, tuna, or salmon Cheese string Hard-boiled egg Natural beef or turkey jerky Greek yogurt	Whole fruit (e.g., banana, apple, orange, peach etc.) Bag of smaller fruits (e.g., strawberries or grapes) Dried fruit (e.g., raisins, apricots etc.) Raw veggies (e.g., carrots, cucumber, bell peppers, sugar snap peas etc.)	Water Milk Fruit juice

Example:

CARBOHYDRATES	PROTEIN	VEGETABLES & FRUIT	DRINK
Two slices of whole-grain bread Granola bar	Sandwich filling: Chicken Greek Yogurt	Sandwich filling: leafy greens Apple	Juice box

The athlete's dinner

Your dinner has two objectives, to help you recover after a hard practice and provide you with nutrition for good health.

Half of your dinner should be "good carbs":

- whole-grain pasta (spaghetti, noodles, penne, macaroni)
- rice (basmati, long grain, brown)
- quinoa, couscous
- potatoes, sweet potatoes, yams

One quarter of your dinner should be lean protein:

- meat (beef, pork, or lamb)
- poultry (chicken or turkey)
- fish (oily or white)
- tofu
- legumes (chick peas, beans, or lentils)

The remaining quarter of your dinner should be vegetables or salad:

- mixed green salad
- carrots, butternut squash
- broccoli, cauliflower, brussel sprouts
- green beans, green peas
- corn
- spinach, kale
- sweet bell peppers
- mushrooms

If you cook your own meals, here are some of my tips. If your meals are prepared for you, you might like to pass these tips on.

As a busy mom, I don't want to spend a long time in the kitchen preparing and cooking meals. I prefer meals that are quick and easy to prepare yet healthy, tasty and meet the needs of my athletic family. I often use my slow cooker, so I can prepare meals in advance when a window of time opens during the day. I love coming home to a cooked meal that is ready and waiting for our family to eat. Also, if anyone in my family must eat at a different time, I set the slow cooker to the 'warm' setting and they serve themselves when it suits them. I also like to prepare double the recipe, so I can freeze the leftovers for a meal on another day. This is great when I have a very busy day and don't have the time to cook or when I simply want a day off from cooking!

Many great slow cooker recipes can be found on the internet and slow cooker cookbooks are available in most grocery stores and bookshops.

Good meals for athletes

- Spaghetti Bolognese made with lean ground beef, tomato-based sauce and extra vegetables (e.g., mushrooms or carrots).
- Noodles with stir fried vegetables, and lean beef, chicken or tofu
- Chicken breast (or any lean meat) with mashed potatoes and vegetables (e.g., broccoli, cauliflower, green beans) and gravy.
- Pasta with a low-fat cheese sauce and canned tuna or salmon and mixed vegetables.
- Rice bowl with chicken breast, tuna, or ham and mixed vegetables (e.g., corn, peas, and bell peppers).
- Chili made with lean ground beef or ground turkey, beans, salsa, served on a bed of rice.
- Deep-crust pizza with lean meat, chicken or tuna and vegetables.
- Large baked potato with lean beef chili, beans, or cheese plus a mixed-green salad.
- Baked salmon (or any fish) with boiled potatoes and steamed greens.

Athletes' meals during training breaks

When you are not training during your summer break, you should change the balance of carbohydrates, proteins, and vegetables on your plate. Your carbohydrate needs are less when you are not training.

- Instead of half of your plate being carbs, only a quarter of your plate should be carbs (e.g., potato, pasta, rice).
- Instead of one quarter of your plate being vegetables or salad, half of your plate should now be vegetables or salad.
- Continue having a quarter of your plate from lean, protein rich foods.

Snacks between meals

As an athlete, it is important for you to eat every two to three hours. Snacks need to be part of your daily food plan because breakfast, lunch, and dinner are at least four to five hours apart.

Your snacks should come mid-morning, mid-afternoon, and just before bed.

Quick, simple, and nutritious snacks include:

- Fresh fruit or a fruit cup.
- Granola bar (see Chapter 11 for recipe).
- Greek yogurt, fruit yogurt.
- Fruit/oatmeal muffin (see Chapter 11 for recipe).
- Cheese and whole-grain crackers.
- Trail mix (see Chapter 11 for recipe).

Choosing a healthy granola-type snack bar

New and different bars are coming onto the market all the time. The guidelines below will help you choose between healthy bars and those that just *appear* healthy.

Check the 'Ingredients' list

- Whole grains should be listed first (e.g., whole oats, whole grain brown rice, whole grain barley).
- Choose bars with only a few ingredients
- Avoid bars that have sugar listed first.
- Avoid bars containing hydrogenated or partially hydrogenated vegetable oils.
- Avoid bars with artificial colours or flavours (or ingredients that you can't pronounce).

Check the 'Nutrition Facts' panel

- Look for bars with 10 grams or less of sugar.
- Look for bars containing 3 grams or more of fibre.
- Look for bars that contain 4 grams or more of protein

Fluids

For good health as well as good athletic performance, it is important that you drink regularly throughout the day. It can be challenging to drink enough fluids, so try and get into the habit of having a water bottle with you, so you can rehydrate wherever you are.

If you are a child athlete, you will probably have a poor sense of thirst and you will need to remind yourself to drink more often.

Good drinks for athletes are water, milk, and 100% juices. You should limit sugary drinks, soft drinks, soda pop, and caffeinated drinks as these provide no nutrition and may also have a dehydrating effect. Remember, you should only be drinking sports drinks when you are training or competing.

Planning your meals and snacks

Not many athletes have the luxury of returning home between practice and school or work; therefore, you need to pack enough food for the full day. The following tables give examples of the food you need depending on how much training you are doing:

For days with morning training only:

ACTIVITY	NUTRITION
Home	1. Pre-training snack
Early-morning practice	2. Water or sports drink during training
	3. Breakfast (may be a packed breakfast at the training facility)
School/Work	4. Morning snack
	5. Lunchbox
	6. After-school snack
Home	7. Dinner at home
	8. Snack before bed

For days with afternoon training only:

ACTIVITY	NUTRITION
Home	1. Breakfast
School/Work	2. Morning snack
	3. Lunchbox
	4. Pre-training snack
Afternoon practice	5. Water or sports drink during training
	6. Post-training snack
Home	7. Dinner at home
	8. Snack before bed

For days with morning and afternoon training:

ACTIVITY	NUTRITION
Home	1. Pre-training snack
Early-morning practice	2. Water or sports drink during training
	3. Breakfast (may be a packed breakfast at the training facility)
School/Work	4. Morning snack
	5. Lunchbox
	6. Pre-training snack
Afternoon practice	7. Water or sports drink during training
	8. Post-training snack
Home	9. Dinner at home
	10. Snack before bed

Understanding food labels

There are two important sets of information on all food packaging: the 'Nutrition Facts' panel and the 'Ingredients' list. These labels are intended to make it easier to assess the nutritional value of foods, manage special diets, compare brands, and choose the right foods.

The Nutrition Facts panel

The 'Nutrition Facts' panel lists the calories and nutrients in one serving of the food. To make sense of the 'Nutrition Facts' panel, it is important to understand what each of the following mean:

Nutrition Facts / Valeur nutritive
Per 1 Cup (250mL) / pour 1 tasse (250 mL)

Amount / Teneur	% Daily Value / % valeur quotidienne
Calories / Calories 80	
Fat/Lipides 0 g	0 %
Saturated / saturés 0 g	0 %
+ Trans / trans 0 g	
Cholesterol / Cholestérol 0 mg	0 %
Sodium / Sodium 10 mg	0 %
Potassium / Potassium 250 mg	7 %
Carbohydrates /Glucides 19 g	6 %
Fibre / Fibres less than 1g	3 %
Sugars / Sucres 16 g	
Protein / Protéines less than 1g	
Vitamin A / Vitamine A	0 %
Vitamin C / Vitamine C	100 %
Calcium / Calcium	0 %
Iron / Fer	2 %

Serving size

The serving size is the first place to start. The serving size is given in familiar household units: cups, tablespoons, or portions of the food (e.g., one slice of bread). You need to think about the amount of the food you typically consume and compare this amount to the serving size. In the example, the serving size is one cup, so if you eat two cups, you must double the numbers for all the nutrients listed.

Always check whether the 'Nutrition Facts' panel refers to the food in its "as-prepared" state or simply as the dry, uncooked ingredient. For example, the calories and nutrients in one cup of cooked rice are very different from one cup of uncooked rice.

Calories

The number of calories listed on the 'Nutrition Facts' panel are the number of calories in one serving of the product. If you have more than one serving of the product, you will consume more calories than listed. In the example, there are 80 calories in one cup of the product, so if you are going to eat 1.5 cups, you will consume 1.5 x 80, or 120 calories.

Fat

The number of grams of 'total fat' in one serving of the product, is the combined amount of saturated, polyunsaturated, monounsaturated, and trans fat. Your goal is to choose foods that contain proportionately more of the healthy fats (monounsaturated and polyunsaturated) and less saturated and trans fats.

For pre-training or pre-competition snacks, I have talked about eating low-fat foods. That means a 'total fat' content of 5 grams or less per serving.

Cholesterol

You don't need to spend too much time considering the cholesterol number. This substance is found in animal foods and has little or no effect on most people's blood cholesterol level. It is far more important to limit sugary carbs, trans fats, and saturated fats if you want to lower your cholesterol level.

Sodium

Sodium (salt) is needed to regulate your fluid balance and blood pressure. It also keeps your muscles and nerves working properly. However, consuming too much salt can lead to high blood pressure, which is a major risk factor for stroke, heart disease, and kidney disease.

The healthy upper daily sodium limit is 2,300 milligrams which is equivalent to just one teaspoon of salt.

Most of the salt we consume each day is hidden in processed, packaged food. To quickly determine if a food has a little or a lot of sodium, read the '% Daily Value'. Foods low in sodium will have a % daily value less than 5%. Foods high in sodium will have a % daily value of 25% or more. It's OK to include high sodium foods in your diet if you balance them with low sodium foods in your meals and snacks. Good examples of low-sodium foods are fresh fruits, fresh vegetables, and fresh (non-processed) meat, poultry and fish.

Carbohydrates

The number of grams of 'total carbohydrate' per serving includes the amount of carbohydrate from dietary fibre and sugars.

Dietary fibre is naturally present in plant-based foods and is resistant to digestion and provides numerous health benefits. For good health, you should eat a total of 25 to 30 grams of fibre every day.

If you suffer from an upset stomach during competition, it is important to choose low-fibre foods for competition snacks and meals (see the next chapter). If this sounds like you, check the label and avoid foods that have more than 5 grams of fibre per serving.

The grams of sugars tell you how much sugar is added to one serving of the product. One teaspoon of sugar is equal to 4 grams of sugars. Snack foods, candy, and soda pop have large amounts of added sugar, for example, a can of soda pop has 40 grams which is equivalent to 10 teaspoons of sugar! If the number of grams of sugar is close to (or the same as) the total number of carbohydrates, the food or drink is a high sugar food or drink. These foods and drinks should only form a small part of your healthy diet as they provide little nutritional benefit.

% daily value

'% daily values' are based on consuming an average diet of 2,000 calories per day. As an athlete, you will consume more than 2,000 calories per day, and some of you will consume significantly more! This means that the % daily values given for calories, carbohydrates, proteins, and fat will be misleading for you. You should therefore ignore these numbers.

The % daily value is most useful to determine whether a food contains a low, good or high amount of a vitamin or mineral.

5% daily value	10% to 19% daily value	20% or more daily value
Low	Good	High

Ingredients list

The 'Ingredients' list provides each ingredient item in descending order of weight. This simply means that the ingredients that weigh the most are listed first and the ingredients that weigh the least are listed last.

Use the list of ingredients to choose products with nutritious ingredients such as whole-grains and healthy fats and to avoid products with unhealthy ingredients such as hydrogenated fats, artificial colours and artificial flavourings. The list of ingredients is also a source of information when you need to avoid certain ingredients due to specific food allergies and intolerances.

Remember if sugar appears high up in the list of ingredients, then it is a high sugar product. Be aware that sugar can be disguised by different names e.g., sucrose, dextrose, glucose, galactose, maltose, maltodextrin, high fructose corn syrup, barley malt, brown rice syrup, molasses syrup, and caramel.

6.
COMPETITION NUTRITION

THE BASICS

Swimming races can be won or lost in as little as one hundredth of a second. Eating right during competition will enable you to race at your very best and could mean the difference between victory and defeat!

Breakfast

You probably won't have much time in the morning before you must be in the pool for warm-up, so choose foods that you can digest quickly and easily.

Your competition-day breakfast should contain mostly carbohydrates with some low-fat protein. Good low-fat protein breakfast foods include: eggs (boiled, poached, or scrambled), lean bacon, low-fat cheese, low-fat milk, and low-fat Greek yogurt.

Good breakfast choices are:

- Whole-grain cereals and low-fat milk (2% or less).
- Oatmeal (made with low fat milk) with added fruit.
- Whole-grain toast and jam with a small amount of nut butter.
- Toast with boiled, poached, or scrambled egg.
- French toast (see recipe in Chapter 11) and fruit.
- Pancakes (see recipe in Chapter 11) with fruit and small amount of lean bacon.
- Low-fat Greek yogurt with fruit and granola.

Don't forget to have a drink with your breakfast to ensure you start the competition well hydrated. 100% juice, milk, herbal fruit teas, and hot chocolate are good choices.

Bad breakfast choices include high-fat, high-protein foods such as fatty bacon, sausages, fried eggs, hash browns, donuts, and pastries. These foods take too long to digest and increase the risk of an upset stomach during warm-up. A large cooked (fried) breakfast can take four to six hours to digest!

Lunch

Usually, you will only have a few hours between the end of the morning preliminary swims and the afternoon finals, so you will need to choose your lunch wisely. Your goal is to top up your energy levels for the evening finals while avoiding indigestion.

You will probably not be able to go home between morning and afternoon sessions, and will need to buy lunch at a nearby restaurant or fast-food outlet. Here are some good lunch options for eating out:

- Subs, wraps, sandwiches with ham or chicken or tuna or egg plus salad and a low-fat dressing.
- Deep-crust pizza with low-fat toppings (ham, chicken, tuna, veggie—NOT the meat feast).
- Grilled chicken burger in a bun.
- Minestrone soup and bread.
- Soft tacos or burritos with rice (limit the guacamole, cheese, and sour cream).
- Rice bowls with lean meat and veggies (boiled rice, not fried).
- Noodles with vegetables, lean meat, or chicken.
- Pasta in a marinara sauce (NOT the high-fat, cream-based sauces).
- Baked potatoes with lean beef chili, beans, or cottage cheese.

If you can go home for lunch or you have a packed lunch, refer to Chapter 5 for good options.

Remember to top up your fluids. Water, milk, flavoured milk, 100% juices, and fruit smoothies are good lunchtime drink choices.

Bad lunch choices include hamburgers, cheeseburgers, hot dogs, battered fish, deep-fried chicken, large portions of fries, large servings of meat, doughnuts, pies, and pastries. These foods are too high in fat or protein and will take hours to digest.

Nutrition between races

To ensure that you keep properly fuelled between races but are not too full to race, you will need to eat the right snack at the right time.

Immediately after each race, drink a few mouthfuls of sports drink and then do your cool-down swim. As soon as you return from your cool-down swim, eat a snack. Decide which snack to eat based on how long you have before your next race.

Pack a variety of foods and drinks from the following list to cover different time intervals between races.

Time to next race	Good snack choice
15 mins or less	Water or sports drinks
15-30 mins	Water or sports drinks 3-4 plain crackers Small handful of pretzels Small handful of low sugar breakfast cereal Small handful of popcorn
30 mins or more	Water or sports drinks Fresh and dried fruit, fruit cup Snack bags with crackers or pretzels Snack bags with breakfast cereal or popcorn Plain cookies Cold baby boiled potatoes Raw baby carrots Raisin or banana bread Granola bar (less than 5 grams of fat) Jam or honey sandwich
1-2 hours or more	Water or sports drinks Half or full bagel with low-fat cream cheese or nut butter Sandwich with low-fat protein (e.g., deli turkey, ham, or low-fat cheese) Low-fat cheese and crackers Low-fat yogurt or Greek yogurt Rice pudding cup Trail mix Hard-boiled egg Turkey or beef jerky Plus, anything from the "30 mins or more" list

Evening meal

Your evening meal will help you recover from your day of racing and fuel your muscles for the next day of competition. To do this best, you need to eat your evening meal as soon as you can after your last race of the day.

Your evening meal should be like a training day dinner. Refer to Chapter 5 for meal ideas, but remember:

- Plenty of carbohydrates: fill half of your plate with pasta, rice, or potatoes.
- Moderate amount of protein: the size and thickness of your palm.
- Good serving of vegetables or salad.

You should drink plenty of fluids (water, juice, or milk) in the hours following the evening swim session to ensure that you replace the fluid you lost during the swim meet.

If you are eating out, remember to pre-plan or order your evening meal so that you can eat quickly and don't have to wait too long for your meal to arrive. After your last race of the swim meet, you have my permission to indulge in anything you want—you deserve it!

THE DETAIL

Introduction

Swim meets create many nutritional challenges. They are often held over several days, with preliminary heats in the morning and finals in the evening. You usually race several times in one day, plus warm-up and cool-down swims. You have limited opportunities to eat and you will probably feel nervous. This combination of factors can hugely impact your food intake. I always get very nervous before and during competition, and must remind myself to eat.

In addition, swim meets are often held in different cities, meaning that you must travel and stay away from home for several days. This can make it even more challenging to eat right, so planning and preparation are essential.

Prior to travel

If you are travelling to a swim meet and staying away from home, it is important to find out the answers to the following questions before you travel:

- Is breakfast available at the hotel and are they open early enough to serve breakfast before warm-up? If not, you must take breakfast food with you or find a restaurant or food outlet that can provide you with suitable breakfast options.
- Does your hotel room have a fridge, freezer, and microwave? If not, you must bring a cooler or take only non-perishable food.
- Which restaurants are situated near the hotel or swimming pool? Eating lunch and dinner soon after your last race of each swim session is important, so you don't want to spend too long looking for a restaurant.

Travelling to a swim meet

You should eat and drink frequently during travel to top up your muscle energy stores and hydration levels. It is important to choose foods that are suitable for travel. Remember to keep your food safe by storing it in insulated lunch boxes or a small cooler. Good travel food choices include:

Sandwiches and wraps	Raw vegetables
Small bag of dry breakfast cereal	Cheese and crackers
Pasta, potato, and rice salads	Trail mix and nuts
Tuna with a flip-top lid	Puréed fruit pouches
Fresh fruit, dried fruit, fruit cup	Granola and cereal bars
Squeezable yogurt	Boiled eggs

It is a good idea to have planned stops during travel that everybody in the car or bus knows about. This will allow you to drink more fluids because you know there will be breaks along the way to use the washroom.

Preparing meals in the hotel room

If there is a small fridge, freezer, and microwave in your hotel room, it is possible to prepare suitable meals. Microwaves can be used to cook oatmeal, scramble eggs, bake potatoes, and heat healthy microwaveable meals. Stack the fridge with fresh fruits, milk, yogurt, raw vegetables, bagels, bread, wraps, cheese, low-fat deli meats, and nut butters for quick, easy meals and snacks.

Breakfast and lunch before warm-up

It is important to eat breakfast before your morning session and lunch before your afternoon swim session.

Your pre-competition meal should:

- be high in carbohydrates;
- contain a moderate amount of protein;
- be low in fat;
- include a drink.

Go back to "The Basics" of this chapter and Chapter 5, "Everyday Meals and Snacks for Athletes" for good breakfast and lunch choices.

Your pre-competition meal should be familiar, easy to digest, and well tolerated. Competition days are NOT the right time to experiment with new foods.

You should avoid eating high-fat, high-protein meals that are difficult to digest and take too long to empty from your stomach. You don't want that bloated, heavy feeling while you are in the water. Also, remember that when food is in your stomach, blood must go there to digest it. If blood is going to your stomach, then there's less blood going to your muscles to power you through a race.

Other foods to avoid are high-sugar foods and drinks like pop, sugary drinks, energy drinks, and candy. High-sugar foods and drinks provide only short lasting energy that's quickly followed by an energy crash and will leave you feeling more tired.

Poor appetite due to nervousness

Poor appetite is common when you are feeling nervous before a swim meet. Sometimes, you can get so nervous that you struggle to eat your pre-competition meal. If this sounds like you, try drinking a liquid meal replacement which is easy to take. Alternatively, you can try eating bland foods such as plain toast, a plain baked potato, or a light breakfast cereal with a little low-fat milk. Another tip is to try eating *little and often*—in other words, eat a small amount of food every twenty minutes or so.

Stomach upsets

Bloating and diarrhea can be a problem for some swimmers. If this sounds like you, avoid high-fibre cereals, legumes (beans, chick peas, and lentils), spicy foods, and excessive amounts of fruits, vegetables, and 100% juices. Good food choices are bland, low- fat, low-fibre foods such as white toast, baked potato, bananas, cornflakes or crisped rice cereal with 1% milk, low-fat yogurts, and sports drinks.

Eating between swimming races

Immediately after your warm up, and immediately after each race, replace fluids by drinking some sports drink or water from your water bottle.

Depending on how much time you have before your next race, choose a suitable snack from the list in "The Basics" earlier in this chapter. Remember to put a cold pack in your snack bag as this will help to keep your food cool and more appealing to eat. Make sure you pack plenty of snacks, both sweet and savoury, and remember to eat the right snack based on how long you have before your next race.

- If there are less than 15 minutes before your next race, just keep to fluid replacement—water or sports drink only.
- If there are 15 to 30 minutes before your next race, eat a small, light carbohydrate snack.
- If there are more than 30 minutes before your next race, you can eat one to two light carbohydrate snacks.
- If there is more than one hour before your next race, use this time to eat more and include some low-fat protein.

Don't forget your fluids

Remember that the indoor pool environment is warm and humid and if you don't drink enough fluids, you can easily become dehydrated. Always have your water bottle handy and drink steadily throughout the swim session rather than drinking large amounts at a time. The key warning signs of dehydration are dizziness, light-headedness, muscle cramps, nausea, and/or headaches. If you have any of these symptoms, sit down and take some fluids immediately.

Evening meal: the "recovery meal"

Your evening meal will help you to recover and prepare your body for the next day of racing. To do this best, you need to eat as soon as possible after the last race of the day. That means planning where you are going to eat, getting there quickly, and being served quickly. If you are eating at a restaurant, you may be able to pre-order by phone. If you are eating at home, have a meal pre-prepared that you can quickly heat up and eat when you arrive home.

Your evening meal should be like a training-day evening meal (see Chapter 5, "Everyday Meals and Snacks for Athletes" for ideas). Planning is important to avoid the high-fat fast foods that will delay your recovery.

Good recovery meal choices include pasta and rice meals with some lean protein (beef, chicken, or fish) and vegetables or salad on the side.

If you are eating out at a restaurant, although it is tempting, avoid meals that contain large slabs of meat like steak, ribs, etc., as they will fill you up with too much protein and do not leave you enough room to eat muscle-refuelling carbohydrate foods. Also, meals containing too much protein and/or fat will prevent you from getting a good night's sleep as your body will be trying to digest the meal through the night. If your meal arrives and there is only a small amount of carbohydrate on your plate, ask the server for some extra bread rolls.

The only exception to these guidelines is after your last race on the last day of the swim meet when you should enjoy whatever meal you like—you deserve it!

7. GAINING MUSCLE MASS

THE BASICS

If you are struggling to keep weight on, or you would like to gain more weight, then you will need to eat more calories than you are currently doing, and for some of you, this will mean eating significantly more calories!

When people want to gain weight, they usually want to increase their muscle mass, not body fat. To increase your muscle mass, it is essential to combine your increased calorie intake with resistance type exercise such as swimming and dryland. This is required to stimulate and create muscle growth. If you increase your calorie intake without any exercise, you will simply store the surplus calories as body fat.

Calories for muscle gain

When you eat food, the number of calories you consume are determined by the amounts of carbohydrate, protein, and fat in that food.

The extra calories that you must consume to build muscle should come from a combination of carbohydrates, fats, and proteins, not just from extra protein. Very high intakes of protein does not build more muscle—a very common misconception.

Increasing your calorie intake
- Plan regular meals and snacks for the day. It is easier to eat more frequently than to increase the size of your existing meals. Aim to have three meals plus multiple snacks each day, including pre- and post-training snacks.
- Keep a food journal to identify the times in a busy day when you are not eating. Eating snacks should become a priority, even during busy days.
- Pack plenty of non-perishable foods and drinks in your backpack for the day ahead e.g., UHT flavoured milk, fruit juice boxes, granola bars, energy bars, crackers and trail mix.
- Choose foods and drinks that provide a compact source of calories and nutrients (for ideas, see the list of high-calorie foods and drinks).

- It is OK for you to include some refined carbs (e.g., white rice) into your diet, especially after training. Whole-grain, high-fibre foods are important for good health, but, eating too many of these foods can make you feel too full and reduce the number of calories that you can eat.
- Always fuel before, during, and after training. Flavoured milks (such as chocolate, strawberry, banana), fruit yogurts, fruit smoothies, and liquid meal supplements provide a compact, easy source of carbohydrate and protein.

Although you must consume a high number of calories, avoid using 'gaining weight' as an excuse to eat junk foods that provide little or no nutrition or "empty calories". The following list of "high-calorie foods and drinks" provide a compact source of calories and nutrition and can be included regularly into your weight gain diet.

High calorie foods and drinks

- Oatmeal cooked with milk and granola type breakfast cereals with milk or yogurt. Add honey, maple syrup, dried fruits, nuts, and seeds for extra calories.
- Chocolate hazelnut spread and nut butters (e.g. peanut butter, and almond butter) provide a high-calorie spread on waffles, toast, bagels, etc.
- Granola bars, fruit/oatmeal muffins, raisin bread, oatmeal and raisin cookies, and trail mix are great snack foods.
- Smoothies (see recipe in Chapter 11), flavoured milks, fruit juices, and meal-replacement drinks – useful before and after training.
- Whole milk and dairy products -avoid the fat free, low calorie, diet products.
- Rice or milk pudding, fruit Greek yogurt, date square, fruit pie and custard, fruit crumble and ice-cream are good dessert choices.
- Healthy fats such as avocados, nuts and seeds added to your meals and snacks e.g., hemp seeds added to your cereal or yogurt.
- Healthy oils added to your meals e.g., drizzle olive oil over vegetables or an olive oil dressing over a salad (avoid the low-calorie salad dressings).

The example below shows how small dietary changes make a significant difference in daily calorie intake.

Daily food and drink intake before dietary changes:	Daily food and drink intake after dietary changes:
Pre-training snack: oatmeal (0.5 cup oats and water) and a glass of juice (250ml)	Pre-training snack: oatmeal (0.5 cup oats) **made with milk (0.75 cup)** and a glass of juice (250ml).
Training: 591 ml (20 oz.) sports drink	Training: 591 ml (20 oz.) sports drink
Breakfast: peanut butter sandwich (two slices) and glass of juice (250ml)	Breakfast: peanut butter **and jam (1tbsp)** sandwich and **glass of milk (250ml)**
Morning snack: granola bar and water	Morning snack: granola bar **plus a banana** and water.
Lunch: ham sandwich, yogurt, orange and water	Lunch: ham **and cheese (1oz)** sandwich, yogurt, orange and **oatmeal raisin cookie** and water
Pre-training snack: cinnamon raisin bagel and glass of 2% milk (250 ml)	Pre-training snack: cinnamon raisin bagel and glass of 2% milk (250ml)
Training: 591 ml (20 oz.) sports drink	Training: 591 ml (20 oz.) sports drink
After training: nothing	After training: **low-fat chocolate milk (500ml)**
Dinner: Beef Bolognese (one cup) and penne pasta (two cups, cooked)	Dinner: Beef Bolognese (one cup) and penne pasta (two cups, cooked) **plus a fruit Greek yogurt**
Bedtime: two slices toast spread with butter (1tbsp) plus a glass 2% milk	Bedtime: two slices of toast spread with **chocolate hazelnut spread (2 tbsp)** plus a glass of 2% milk
TOTAL 3,500 CALORIES	**TOTAL 4,500 CALORIES**

Be patient and realistic

Remember that muscle development takes time. To build muscle, you should:

- Set a realistic goal in view of your genetics. By looking at the physical build of your family members, this will give you an indication of what you can realistically achieve.
- Give yourself enough time to achieve your goal. It may take several months, but if you consistently increase your daily calorie intake, you will see the results.
- Give your body a complete rest day from training each week and get enough sleep every night. Your body repairs and builds muscle when you are resting.

THE DETAIL

If you are following the advice in 'The Basics' but you are still struggling to gain weight, then you may want to try a more detailed plan of action. In 'The Detail', you will learn more about:

- your personal daily calorie burn;
- how to adjust your daily calorie intake to achieve weight gain;
- how much carbohydrate, protein, and fat you need to consume each day.

Step-by-step approach

There are five steps to follow if you want a more detailed approach to understanding your daily calorie needs and adjusting your eating habits:

1. Use specific equations to calculate the number of calories you burn each day.
2. Use one of the many available websites or apps to track your usual calorie intake. Input your usual food and drink consumption for several days to get your average daily calorie intake. Compare your average daily calorie intake with your daily calorie burn. This will tell you how many more calories you will need to eat each day.

3. Use the information from 'The Basics' of this chapter to increase your daily calorie intake.
4. Keep track of your calorie intake using a website or app to make sure that you are hitting your calorie target on a regular basis.
5. Use the website or app to check that you are eating the correct amounts of carbohydrates, protein, and fat.

In this chapter, I have also included a detailed case study to show how each of these steps work.

What are calories?

Your body burns calories every day to perform the basic functions of life: breathing, pumping blood, processing food, repairing cells, and growing. Even when you are asleep, your body is burning calories. You also burn calories doing your everyday activities at school or work or home. On top of all that, you burn even more calories when you are training.

You consume calories every time you eat and drink. The calories in food and drink are determined by the amounts of carbohydrates, protein, and fat in that food or drink. Foods and drinks contain a combination of carbohydrates, protein, and fat in different proportions. For example:

- Bread: mostly carbs some protein a little fat
- Chicken: no carbs mostly protein some fat
- Avocado: some carbs a little protein mostly fat

How many calories do you need to gain muscle mass?

For a steady weight gain of up to one pound (0.5 kg) per week, you will need to consume an extra 500 to 1,000 calories each day.

Let's look at the five-step process in more detail:

1. Estimate your personal daily calorie burn and work out your calorie target for weight gain.
2. Estimate your usual calorie intake.

3. Use the information in "The Basics" to increase your usual calorie intake.
4. Keep track to make sure you are hitting your calorie target for weight gain.
5. Eat the right amounts of carbohydrates, protein, and fat (macronutrients).

Step 1: estimate your daily calorie burn

Your daily calorie burn depends on many variables:

- **Your height and weight.** The bigger you are; the more calories you burn moving your body.
- **Your gender.** The more muscle mass you have, the more calories you will burn. In general, men have more muscle mass than women.
- **Your age.** You burn more calories when you are growing. Teenagers going through a growth spurt burn more calories.
- **How active you are in your daily life.** You burn more calories if you have an active lifestyle outside of your swimming.
- **The number of hours of training.** The more hours you train each day, the more calories you will burn.
- **How hard you train.** The more effort you put into your training, the more calories you will burn.

I use the Estimated Energy Requirement (EER) calculation, which estimates your daily calorie burn based on your age, gender, weight, height, and level of physical activity (PA).

You will see below that there are different equations depending on your age and gender. Even though the equations will give you a precise number of calories, predicting your daily calorie burn is not a precise science and the equations should be used as a guideline only.

You will need to input:

- Your age in years
- Your weight in kilograms (divide weight in pounds by 2.2)
- Your height in metres (multiply height in inches by 0.0254)
- Your PA number (see the table and explanation later)

Boys 9-18 years

Daily calorie burn = 88.5 - 61.9 x age [y] + PA x {(26.7 x weight [kg]) + (903 x height [m])} +25

Girls 9-18 years

Daily calorie burn = 135.3 - (30.8 x age [y]) + PA x {(10.0 x weight [kg]) + (934 x height [m])} + 25

Men 19 years and older

Daily calorie burn = 662 - (9.53 x age [y]) + PA x {(15.91 x weight [kg]) + (539.6 x height [m])}

Women 19 years and older

Daily calorie burn = 354 - (6.91 x age [y]) + PA x {(9.36 x weight [kg]) + (726 x height [m])}

Physical Activity numbers for use in the calculation:

Boys 9-18 years:		Girls 9-18 years:	
Sedentary:	1.0	Sedentary:	1.0
Low active:	1.13	Low active:	1.16
Active:	1.26	Active:	1.31
Very active:	1.42	Very active:	1.56
Men 19 years and older:		Women 19 years and older:	
Sedentary:	1.0	Sedentary:	1.0
Low active:	1.11	Low active:	1.12
Active:	1.25	Active:	1.27
Very active:	1.48	Very active:	1.45

Sedentary means that you do light everyday activities such as sitting, walking short distances, and light household tasks.

Low active means that you do the typical sedentary activities (as above) *PLUS* you exercise for 30 to 60 minutes each day.

Active means that you do the typical sedentary activities (as above) *PLUS* you exercise for 60 to 90 minutes each day.

Very active means that you do the typical sedentary activities (as above) *PLUS* you exercise for 90 to 120 minutes each day.

Once you have worked out your daily calorie burn, you will need to add at least 500 calories to give you the number of calories you must consume each day to gain weight.

Please note that if you have a very active lifestyle (such as a manual job) outside of your swimming, or you regularly train for more than two hours each day, the equations will underestimate your daily calorie burn. Consider working with a registered dietitian who specializes in sports nutrition for a more realistic daily calorie target.

Step 1: Case study

Let's see how these equations work by looking at an example case study:

Bob is a sixteen-year-old male student who weighs 150 pounds (68 kg) and is 5'10" (1.8 m) tall. He would like to gain more muscle mass. His goal weight is 155 pounds.

*He trains for 2-hours, six days of the week and is classed as "very active." His **PA = 1.42**.*

Using the equation for boys 9-18 years old, we calculate the following:

Daily calorie burn

= 88.5 − (61.9 x Age) + [PA x (26.7 x Wt) + (903 x Ht)] +25

= 88.5 − **(61.9 x Age)** + [PA x (26.7 x Wt) + (903 x Ht)] +25
  61.9 x Age
  61.9 x 16
  990

= 88.5 − (61.9 x Age) + [PA x **(26.7 x Wt)** + (903 x Ht)] +25
  26.7 x Wt
  26.7
  x 68
  1,816

$= 88.5 - (61.9 \times Age) + [PA \times (26.7 \times Wt) + \mathbf{(903 \times Ht)}] + 25$

$903 \times Ht$

903×1.8

1,625

$= 88.5 - (61.9 \times Age) + [PA \times (26.7 \times Wt) + (903 \times Ht)] + 25$

$= 88.5 - 990 + [\mathbf{1.42} \times (1{,}816 + 1{,}625)] + 25$

$= 88.5 - 990 + [1.42 \times 3{,}441] + 25$

$= 88.5 - 990 + 4{,}886 + 25$

$= \mathbf{4{,}010}$

In other words, Bob burns about 4,000 calories each day.

So, for Bob to gain muscle mass, he must consume a minimum of 4,500 calories each day.

Step 2: Estimating your usual calorie intake

There are many good websites and apps on the market (quite a lot of them are free) that you can use to track your calorie intake. They make this task simple because they already contain a huge amount of information on the foods and drinks that we buy.

Even though these websites and apps do most of the hard work for you, it is still very important to be specific when you input the information. Get into the habit of recording everything you eat and drink when you have it. That way, you won't be relying on your memory when you input the information into your chosen website or app.

You should track your food and drink intake for a minimum of three days to give yourself a good idea of your usual daily consumption. Make sure that you choose days that are typical for you, in terms of your training and usual meals and snacks.

Once you have a good idea of your usual calorie intake, compare it to your target (from Step 1) to see how many calories you are falling short.

Step 2: Case study

Our sixteen-year-old swimmer Bob downloads a calorie-counting app onto his phone and uses it to record his food intake for three days of regular training and school activities.

At the end of the three days, he reviews his results and finds out that a typical day looks like this:

***Pre-training snack**: oatmeal (0.5 cup oats and water) and a glass of juice (250ml)*

***Training**: 591 ml (20 oz) sports drink*

***Breakfast**: peanut butter sandwich (two slices) and juice box (250 ml)*

***Morning snack**: granola bar and water*

***Lunch**: ham sandwich (2 slices bread, butter and 3 slices of ham), fruit yogurt, orange and water*

***Pre-training snack**: cinnamon raisin bagel and glass of 2% milk (250 ml)*

***Training**: 591 ml (20 oz) sports drink*

***After training**: nothing*

***Dinner**: beef bolognese (one cup) and penne pasta (two cups cooked)*

***Bedtime**: two slices toast spread with butter (1tbsp) plus a glass 2% milk*

His app tells him that him that a typical day provides 3,500 calories.

Bob compares this against 4,500 calories needed to gain weight (from Step 1) and realizes that he must increase his daily intake by 1,000 calories.

Step 3: Use 'The Basics' to increase your daily calorie intake

The information in "The Basics" from this chapter provides you with great ways to increase your calorie intake.

Plan on a course of action to increase your calorie intake and stick with it.

Step 3: Case study

> Bob looks at his usual food and drink choices and decides to make the following changes:
>
> 1. For pre-training snack, he makes his oatmeal with milk instead of water.
> 2. For breakfast, he adds jam to his peanut butter sandwich.
> 3. For morning snack, he includes a banana with the granola bar.
> 4. For lunch, he adds cheese to the ham sandwich and includes an oatmeal raisin cookie.
> 5. For post training snack, he drinks a low-fat chocolate milk instead of having nothing.
> 6. For dinner, he has a fruit Greek yogurt for dessert.
> 7. For bedtime, he puts chocolate hazelnut spread instead of butter on his toast.

Step 4: Keep track to make sure that you are hitting your calorie target

Once you have decided on your new course of action, make the changes and keep track. It is important that you continue to monitor what you are eating and drinking throughout the day to make sure that changes to your eating routine are becoming a habit. We tend to fall back into our old ways of doing things until we get used to new habits.

Keeping track will also help you see whether you need to make more adjustments to your calorie intake to hit your target.

Once you are in a good routine and regularly hitting your calorie target, it is not necessary to keep daily track of your calories. Just check occasionally to make sure you are not slipping back into your old ways.

Step 4: Case study

Bob's modified eating plan for weight gain:

Pre-training snack: oatmeal (0.5 cup oats made with ¾ cup 2% milk) and a glass of juice (250ml)

Training: 591 ml (20 oz.) sports drink

Breakfast: peanut butter and jam (1tbsp) sandwich (two slices) and juice box (250 ml)

Morning snack: granola bar plus a banana and water

Lunch: ham sandwich (2 slices buttered bread, 3 slices of ham and 1oz cheese), fruit yogurt, orange plus oatmeal raisin cookie and water

Pre-training snack: cinnamon raisin bagel and glass of 2% milk (250 ml)

Training: 591 ml (20 oz.) sports drink

After training: low-fat chocolate milk (500ml)

Dinner: beef bolognese (one cup) and penne pasta (two cups cooked) plus a fruit Greek yogurt (150g)

Bedtime: two slices toast spread with chocolate hazelnut spread (2 tbsp) and a glass 2% milk

*Bob records his new food and drink intake using the same app on his phone. It tells him that his new eating plan provides **4,500 calories per day**. He can now be confident that he has sufficiently increased his calorie intake to gain muscle mass.*

Step 5: Eat carbs, protein, and fat (macronutrients) in the correct proportions

Now that you know how many calories you should be eating each day, you need to check that you are eating the right amounts of carbohydrates, fat, and protein within your calorie budget.

To support your training needs and achieve muscle gain, you should consume:

- 60 to 65% of your daily calories from carbohydrates;
- 15 to 20% of your daily calories from protein;
- 20 to 25% of your daily calories from fat.

It gets a bit more complicated, however, as:

- 1 g of carbs provides 4 calories;
- 1 g of protein provides 4 calories;
- 1 g of fat provides 9 calories.

Luckily, your calorie-counting website or app will be able to provide you with all this information and should give you the percentages, as well.

Again, don't get too worried if your percentages are slightly off. You may need to tweak your diet a few times before you are eating the right number of calories and the correct amounts of carbs, protein, and fat. Once you have established what works for you, stick with it. You should only re-check your calorie intake or percentages occasionally or when you make more changes to your diet.

Step 5: Case study

Bob's new dietary plan provides 4,500 calories, 700 g carbohydrates, 180 g protein and 110 g fat:

Carbs: (Bob needs 60-65% of his calories from carbohydrate)
700g carbohydrate is 700 multiplied by 4 = 2,800 calories
2,800 divided by 4,500 multiplied by 100 = 62%

Protein: (Bob needs 15-20% of his calories from protein)
180g protein is 180 multiplied by 4 = 720 calories
720 divided by 4,500 multiplied by 100 = 16%

Fat: (Bob needs 20-25% of his calories from fat)
110 g fat is 110 multiplied by 9 = 990 calories
990 divided by 4,500 multiplied by 100 = 22%

At 62% carbs, 16% protein, and 22% fat, Bob's new dietary plan is in the correct range for all three macronutrients.

Monitoring your progress

It is a good idea to monitor your progress through pictures and body measurements.

By taking monthly photographs of your physique, you will see a gradual change over time. In addition, track changes in your measurements of your chest, waist, upper arms, and thighs. Measurements should be taken monthly with a tape measure, at the same spot, and by the same person every time.

Be wary of the bathroom scales. Weight fluctuations are mostly due to changes in body water. You will weigh less when you are dehydrated, especially after a workout, and weigh more when you are fully hydrated. Also, you will weigh several pounds less when you have low muscle glycogen stores and weigh more when you have full muscle glycogen stores (this is because carbohydrate binds to water when it is stored as glycogen). Finally, you will weigh less after emptying your bladder and bowels and weigh more if you have not emptied them for a while!

Bottom line, remember that the bathroom scales only show your weight change and do not tell you how much is due to changes in muscle mass, body fat, and body water.

8.
LOSING BODY FAT

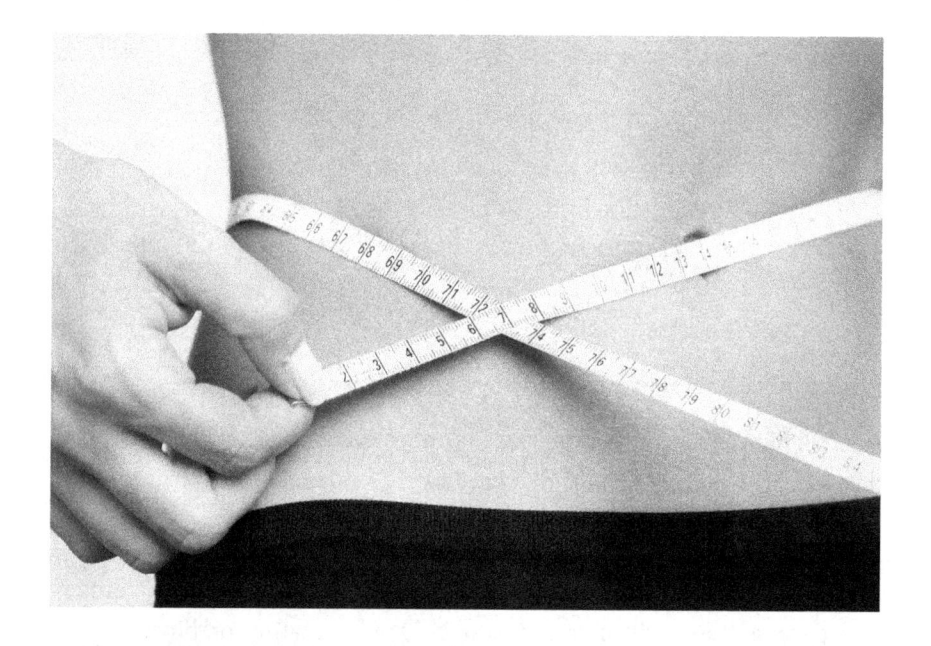

THE BASICS

When people say, "they want to lose weight", what they really mean is, "they want to lose body fat". Your weight comes from muscles, bones, organs, other tissues, water, and fat. To lose body fat, it is important you do it the right way, so that you don't lose important lean muscle tissue.

Before embarking on a weight-loss program, you should consider the following:

77

- Do you need to lose body fat?
- Will a reduction in body fat improve your swimming performance?
- What is a realistic weight for you?

You should discuss these questions with your coach (and parents) and you may also need to talk with your family doctor. If it is agreed that you would benefit from losing some body fat, it is important that you follow an eating plan that provides you with enough calories and nutrients to sustain hard training and support good health. If you reduce your daily calorie intake too much, your swimming performance and health will suffer.

Losing body fat successfully

For successful, long-term body fat loss, you need to:

- learn how to make healthy food choices for meals and snacks;
- eat the right portion sizes for meals and snacks;
- eat at the right times of the day;
- make healthy, life-long changes;
- target slow, steady weight loss.

A healthy rate of fat loss is up to one pound (0.5 kg) per week.

A small but regular reduction in the number of calories you consume each day will make a significant difference to your body fat loss over time.

Low calorie diets lead to failure

Reducing your daily calorie intake too much will leave you feeling hungry and deprived and will increase your risk of overeating or binge eating. Another downside is that you will be training with low or empty muscle energy (glycogen) stores and you will not be able to train hard. Low calorie diets cause you to break down muscle tissue to supply your body with much-needed energy. This means that your muscle mass will reduce and you will have less power in the water.

Although low calorie diets achieve a large, rapid weight loss initially, they give you a false impression of success because most of this weight loss is water. Furthermore, low calorie diets are not sustainable in the long term and when you return to your usual diet, you will quickly put all the weight back on, plus more. This is because low calorie diets cause your body to lose muscle mass which reduces your daily calorie burn. When you return to your usual calorie intake, you easily gain body fat plus more. In other words, "you diet yourself fatter"!

Low-carb diets are not for competitive swimmers

Low-carbohydrate diets have become very popular; however, I do not recommend them for swimmers. Carbohydrates are essential for you to train at a high intensity and if you train with low or empty muscle energy stores, your performance will suffer.

Another drawback to low-carbohydrate diets is that whole grains, fruit, legumes, and vegetables are restricted which deprives you of valuable sources of fibre and micronutrients essential for good health.

First steps

Before you start with your weight-loss program, write down what you eat and drink for several days and see if there is anything that may be contributing to your excess weight. I'm not talking about counting calories, just making a note of your eating habits. For example, are you eating most your food in the evening? Are you skipping pre-and post-training snacks and overeating later? Are you having too many high-calorie, sugary foods and drinks? Are you eating high-calorie snack foods like chips and chocolate bars more often than you think?

Reducing your daily calorie intake may be as simple as cutting out high-sugar drinks or making better snack choices. The following suggestions will help you reduce your calorie intake while maintaining your energy levels for training.

Tips for healthy, effective weight loss

- Never skip a meal. Always eat three healthy, well-balanced meals every day.
- Spread your calorie intake throughout the day. If you eat too little during the day, you will become too hungry and this will lead to overeating at night. Keep your evening meal equal in size to your breakfast and lunch and avoid late night snacking.

- Plan your day's food intake. Prepare and pack appropriate meals and snacks rather than relying on cafeterias and fast-food outlets. That way, you can control your portion size.
- Use low-fat cooking methods like steaming, boiling, broiling, baking, or sautéing in a small amount of healthy oil.
- Include high-fibre carbohydrate foods such as oatmeal, dense wholegrain breads, all types of beans, chickpeas, lentils, sweet potatoes, 100% whole-grain pasta, and quinoa regularly in your meals. These foods help to sustain your energy level and your appetite for longer.
- Eat lean, well-trimmed meats and skinless poultry. Limit fatty meat products such as sausages, hot dogs, beef burgers, bacon, and salami as they are high in fat and calories.
- Eat a large serving of vegetables or salad with your meal. This will increase the volume of food on your plate and help you to feel more satisfied.
- Avoid deep-fried foods such as fried potatoes, fried chicken, and fried fish.
- Avoid the creamy, cheese-based pasta sauces (e.g. alfredo) as these are very high in calories. Choose the tomato-based sauces instead (e.g. marinara).
- Eat your meals slowly by chewing your food well. The quicker you eat, the more food you will be able to eat before your brain receives the signal that you are full and need to stop eating.
- Include some protein or fat in your snacks to satisfy your appetite between meals. Good snack choices include fruit plus a yogurt, whole-grain crackers and cheese, a handful of dried fruit and nuts, or a serving of fruit and a spoonful of nut butter.
- Do not deprive yourself of your favourite foods as this will cause you to crave them and increase your risk of overeating or binge eating. Give yourself permission to include two to three treat foods each week into your diet.
- Be careful when buying muffins. Some muffins in grocery stores and coffee shops can be as high as 600 calories! Choose smaller,

wholegrain, fruit muffins or try baking your own. See Chapter 11 for a healthy, reduced calorie muffin recipe.
- Limit sugary drinks, pop, energy drinks. They are high in sugar and empty calories. Limit fruit juice to one glass per day.
- Drink plenty of water throughout the day and stay well hydrated. Sometimes thirst can be mistaken for hunger.
- Be careful when buying granola bars. Some are loaded with sugar and hydrogenated oils and are high in calories. Look at the ingredients list, if sugar is listed first, then avoid it. See chapter 11 for a healthy, granola bar recipe.
- Be careful when buying yogurt. You will need to read the labels carefully, as some are loaded with fat, sugar, and calories. Choose a reduced fat (2% or less) yogurt with no more than ten grams of added sugar. Better still, try non-fat plain Greek yogurt and sweeten it with fruit (frozen berries put in the microwave for a few seconds create a nice sweet syrup). Try adding a sprinkle of cinnamon and cocoa powder for extra sweetness without the calories.
- Avoid diet food products. Although diet food products have fewer calories than the original product, many cause a rapid spike in blood sugar, followed by an energy crash which leads to hunger and overeating later. Bottom line, stick to eating one serving of the original food product as it is more satisfying and better for your waistline!
- Avoid diet drinks. Although diet drinks contain zero calories, studies have shown that they cause weight gain, not weight loss. The very sweet taste of the artificial sweeteners causes the brain to produce hunger signals because it has not received the calories it was expecting. This stimulates your appetite and causes overeating later. Try sparkling water sweetened with a small amount of 100% fruit juice for a healthy, low-calorie fizzy drink.

THE DETAIL

If you are following the advice in 'The Basics' but are still struggling to lose body fat, then you may want to try a more detailed plan of action. In 'The Detail', you will learn more about:

- your personal daily calorie burn;
- how to adjust your daily calorie intake to achieve body fat loss;
- how much carbohydrate, protein, and fat you need to consume each day.

Assessing whether you are overweight

The body mass index (BMI) formula is a useful first tool for working out whether you are overweight. If your BMI falls between 18.5 and 24.9, your weight is in the healthy range. If your BMI is above 25, you are classed as overweight.

Please note that a BMI of more than 25 can be calculated for an athlete who is lean and very muscular. If your BMI is above 25, you must consider whether your higher BMI is due to your muscular build rather than excess body fat.

BMI = weight in kilograms divided by (height in metres multiplied by height in metres).

Convert your weight in pounds to kilograms by dividing your weight by 2.2. For example, if you weigh 150 pounds, then your weight in kg is 150 divided by 2.2 = 68 kg.

Convert your height in inches to metres by multiplying your height by 0.025. For example, if you are 5'10", which is 70 inches, then 70 x 0.025 = 1.75 m.

In this example, BMI = 68 divided by (1.75 multiplied by 1.75) = 22.2 which is within the healthy weight range.

Again, you should discuss your weight with your coach or doctor before starting a weight-loss program.

Step-by-step approach

There are five steps to follow if you want a more detailed approach to understanding your daily calorie needs and adjusting your eating habits:

1. Use specific equations to calculate the number of calories you burn each day.
2. Use one of the many available websites or apps to track your usual calorie intake. Input your usual food and drink consumption for several days to get your average daily calorie intake. Compare your average daily calorie intake with your daily calorie burn. This will tell you how many calories you will need to reduce each day.
3. Use the information from 'The Basics' of this chapter to decrease your daily calorie intake.
4. Keep track of your calorie intake using a website or app to make sure that you are hitting your calorie target on a regular basis.
5. Use the website or app to check that you are eating the correct amounts of carbohydrates, protein, and fat.

In this chapter, I have also included a detailed case study to show how each of these steps work.

What are calories?

Your body burns calories every day to perform the basic functions of life: breathing, pumping blood, processing food, repairing cells, and growing. Even when you are asleep, your body is burning calories. You also burn calories doing your everyday activities at school or work or home. On top of all that, you burn even more calories when you are training.

You consume calories every time you eat and drink. The calories in food and drink are determined by the amounts of carbohydrates, protein, and fat in that food or drink. Foods and drinks contain a combination of carbohydrates, protein, and fat in different proportions. For example:

- Bread: mostly carbs   some protein   a little fat
- Chicken: no carbs   mostly protein   some fat
- Avocado: some carbs   a little protein mostly fat

How many calories do you need to lose body fat?

To lose body fat rather than muscle, you should aim for a steady weight loss of up to one pound (0.5 kg) per week. In terms of calories, that means you need to consume around 500 calories fewer than you burn each day.

So, if you calculate the number of calories that you burn each day and subtract 500 calories from it, you will have your daily calorie target for weight loss.

Let's look at the five-step process in more detail.

1. Estimate your personal daily calorie burn and work out your calorie target for steady weight loss.
2. Estimate your usual calorie intake.
3. Use the information in 'The Basics' to decrease your usual calorie intake.
4. Keep track to make sure you are hitting your calorie target for weight loss.
5. Eat the right amounts of carbohydrates, protein, and fat (macronutrients).

Step 1: estimate your daily calorie burn

Your daily calorie burn depends on many variables:

- **Your height and weight.** The bigger you are; the more calories you burn moving your body.

- **Your gender.** The more muscle mass you have, the more calories you will burn. In general, men have more muscle mass than women.
- **Your age.** You burn more calories when you are growing. Teenagers going through a growth spurt burn more calories.
- **How active you are in your daily life.** You burn more calories if you have an active lifestyle outside of your swimming.
- **The number of hours of training.** The more hours you train each day, the more calories you burn.
- **How hard you train.** The more effort you put into your training, the more calories you will burn.

I use the Estimated Energy Requirement (EER) calculation, which estimates your daily calorie burn based on your age, gender, weight, height, and level of physical activity (PA).

You will see below that there are different equations depending on your age and gender. Even though the equations will give you a precise number of calories, predicting your daily calorie burn is not a precise science and so the equations should be used as a guideline only.

You will need to input:

- Your age in years
- Your weight in kilograms (divide weight in pounds by 2.2)
- Your height in metres (multiply height in inches by 0.0254)
- Your PA number (see the table and explanation later)

Boys 9-18 years

Daily calorie burn = 88.5 - 61.9 x age [y] + PA x {(26.7 x weight [kg]) + (903 x height [m])} +25

Girls 9-18 years

Daily calorie burn = 135.3 - (30.8 x age [y]) + PA x {(10.0 x weight [kg]) + (934 x height [m])} + 25

Men 19 years and older

Daily calorie burn = 662 - (9.53 x age [y]) + PA x {(15.91 x weight [kg]) + (539.6 x height [m])}

Women 19 years and older

Daily calorie burn = 354 - (6.91 x age [y]) + PA x {(9.36 x weight [kg]) + (726 x height [m])}

Physical Activity numbers for use in the calculation:

Boys aged 9-18:		Girls aged 9-18	
Sedentary:	1.0	Sedentary:	1.0
Low active:	1.13	Low active:	1.16
Active:	1.26	Active:	1.31
Very active:	1.42	Very active:	1.56
Men 19 years and older		**Women 19 years and older**	
Sedentary:	1.0	Sedentary:	1.0
Low active:	1.11	Low active:	1.12
Active:	1.25	Active:	1.27
Very active:	1.48	Very active:	1.45

Sedentary means that you do light everyday activities such as sitting, walking short distances, and light household tasks.

Low active means that you do the typical sedentary activities (as above) *PLUS* you exercise for 45 to 60 minutes each day.

Active means that you do the typical sedentary activities (as above) *PLUS* you exercise for 60 to 90 minutes each day.

Very active means that you do the typical sedentary activities (as above) *PLUS* you exercise for 90 to 120 minutes each day.

Once you have worked out your daily calorie burn, you will need to subtract 500 calories to give you the number of calories you must consume each day to lose weight.

Please note that if you have a very active lifestyle (such as a manual job) outside of your swimming, or you regularly train for more than two hours each day, the equations will underestimate your daily calorie burn. Consider working with a registered dietitian who specializes in sports nutrition for a more realistic daily calorie target.

Step 1: Case study

Let's see how these equations work by looking at an example case study:

Jane is an eighteen-year-old female student who weighs 140 pounds (63.6 kg) and is 5'3" (1.60 m) tall. Her BMI is 24.8 kg/m². Her BMI is at the upper end of the ideal weight range and she would like to lose some body fat. Her goal weight is 130 pounds (59.0kg) and BMI of 23 kg/m².

She trains for 2-hours, six days of the week and is classed as "very active." Her PA = 1.56.

Using the equation for girls aged nine to eighteen years

Daily calorie burn

= 135.3 − (30.8 x Age) + [PA x (10.0 x Weight) + (934 x Height)] + 25

= 135.3 − ***30.8 x Age*** + [PA x (10.0 x Weight) + (934 x Height)] +25
  30.8 x Age
  30.8 x 18
  554.4

= 135.3 − 30.8 x Age + [PA x ***(10.0 x Weight)*** + (934 x Height)] +25
  10.0 x Weight
  10.0 x 63.6
  636.3

= 135.3 − 30.8 x Age + [PA x (10.0 x Weight) + ***(934 x Height)***] +25
  934 x Height
  934 x 1.60
  1,494.6

Daily calorie burn

$= 135.3 - (30.8 \times Age) + [PA \times (10.0 \times Weight) + (934 \times Height)] + 25$

$= 135.3 - 554.4 + [1.56 \times (636.3 + 1494.6)] + 25$

$= 135.3 - 554.4 + [1.56 \times 2130.9] + 25$

$= 135.3 - 554.4 + 3324.2 + 25$

$= 2930.2$

In other words, Jane burns about 2,900 calories each day.

So, for Jane to lose body fat, she must reduce her intake to 2,400 calories each day.

Step 2: Estimate your usual calorie intake

There are many good websites and apps on the market (quite a lot of which are free) that you can use to track your calorie intake. They make this task simple because they already contain a huge amount of information on the foods and drinks that we buy.

Even though these websites and apps do most of the hard work for you, it is still very important to be specific when you input the information. Get into the habit of recording everything you eat and drink when you have it. That way, you won't be relying on your memory when you input the information into your chosen website or app.

You should track your food and drink for a minimum of three days to get a good idea of your usual daily consumption. Make sure that you choose days that are typical for you, in terms of your training and usual meals and snacks.

Once you have a good idea of your usual calorie intake, compare it to your target (from Step 1) to see how many calories you need to reduce.

Step 2: Case study

Our fifteen-year-old swimmer Jane downloads a calorie-counting app onto her phone and uses it to record her food intake for three days of regular training and school activities.

At the end of the three days, she reviews her results and finds out that a typical day looks like this:

Breakfast: *cornflakes (2 cups) with 2% milk (3/4 cup), glass of apple juice (250 ml)*

Morning snack: *cookies (x 3) and juice box (200 ml)*

Lunch: *ham sandwich, small bag of chips, granola bar and a juice box (200ml)*

Mid-afternoon snack: *chocolate milk (250 ml) and raisin bread (2 slices)*

During training: *sports drink (750 ml)*

After training: *juice box (200 ml)*

Dinner: *fried chicken breast with oven fries (2 cups) and Caesar salad (1 cup)*

Bedtime: *chocolate chip cookies (x 3 small) and glass of 2% milk (1 cup)*

Her app tells her that her that a typical day provides 3,000 calories

Jane compares this against 2,400 calories needed to lose weight (from Step 1) and realizes that she must reduce her daily intake by 600 calories.

Step 3: Use 'The Basics' to decrease your daily calorie intake

The information in 'The Basics' from this chapter provides you with great ways to reduce the number of calories in your diet.

Plan on a course of action to reduce your calorie intake and stick with it.

Step 3: Case study

> Jane has a look at her usual food and drink intake and decides to make the following changes:
>
> 1. For breakfast, she eats oatmeal instead of cornflakes as it contains more fibre and will help to satisfy her appetite and sustain her energy levels during the morning.
> 2. For morning snack, she eats whole-grain crackers and cheese instead of cookies. She drinks water instead of a juice box.
> 3. For lunch, she eats a bag of raw veggies instead of a bag of chips.
> 4. For mid afternoon snack, she drinks a glass of low-fat milk instead of chocolate milk.
> 5. For post-training, she swaps the apple juice for low-fat chocolate milk, which will provide her with some protein as well as carbohydrates to refuel and repair her muscles after training.
> 6. For dinner, she has grilled chicken breast instead of fried chicken, a baked potato with low-fat sour cream instead of fries and a reduced calorie dressing on her salad.
> 7. For bedtime, she swaps the chocolate chip cookies and milk for non-fat, plain Greek yogurt and berries.

Step 4: Keep track to make sure that you are hitting your calorie targets

Once you have decided on your new course of action, make the changes and keep track. It is important that you continue to monitor what you are eating and drinking throughout the day to make sure that changes to your eating routine are becoming a habit. We tend to fall back into our old ways of doing things until we get used to new habits.

Keeping track will also help you see whether you need to make more adjustments to your calorie intake (either up or down) to hit your target.

Once you are in a good routine and regularly hitting your calorie target, it is not necessary to keep daily track of your calories. Just re-check occasionally to make sure you are not slipping back into your old ways.

Step 4: Case study

Jane's modified eating plan for weight loss:

Breakfast: *oatmeal (0.5 cup oats and 0.5 cup 2% milk) and 1 cup (250ml) 100% juice*

Morning snack: *cheese (1oz) and wholegrain crackers (x4) and water*

Lunch: *ham sandwich on whole grain, bag of raw veggies, and granola bar and a juice box*

Mid-afternoon/pre-training snack: *two slices of raisin bread and one cup (250ml) of 2% milk*

During training: *700 ml sports drink*

After training: *300ml low-fat chocolate milk*

Dinner: *grilled chicken breast with medium-sized baked potato with low-fat sour cream and mixed green salad with reduced calorie dressing (two tablespoons)*

Bedtime: *0.75 cup of non-fat Greek yogurt sweetened with 0.5 cup of berries*

Jane records her new food and drink intake using the same app on her phone. It tells her that her new eating plan provides **2,400 calories per day**. *She can now be confident that she has sufficiently reduced her calorie intake to lose body fat.*

Step 5: Eat carbs, protein, and fat (macronutrients) in the correct proportions

Now that you know how many calories you should be eating each day, you need to check that you are eating the right amounts of carbohydrates, fat, and protein within your calorie budget.

To support your training needs and achieve weight loss, you should consume:

- 50 to 55% of your daily calories from carbohydrates;
- 15 to 20% of your daily calories from protein;
- 25 to 30% of your daily calories from fat.

It gets a bit more complicated, however, as:

- 1 g of carbs provides four calories;
- 1 g of protein provides four calories;
- 1 g of fat provides nine calories.

Luckily, your calorie-counting website or app will be able to provide you with all this information, and should give you the percentages, as well.

Again, don't get too worried if your percentages are slightly off. You may need to tweak your diet a few times before you are eating the right number of calories and the correct amounts of carbohydrates, protein, and fat. Once you have established what works for you, stick with it. You should only re-check your calorie intake or percentages occasionally or when you make more changes to your diet

Step 5: Case study

Jane's new dietary plan provides 2,400 calories, 330 carbs, 120 g protein, and 67 g fat

Carbohydrate: (Jane needs 50-55% of her calories from carbohydrate)

330 g carbohydrate is 330 multiplied by 4 = 1,320 calories

1,320 divided by 2,400 multiplied by 100 = 55%

Protein: (Jane needs 15-20% of her calories from protein)

120 g protein is 120 multiplied by 4 = 480 calories

480 divided by 2,400 multiplied by 100 = 20%

Fat: (Jane needs 25-30% of her calories from fat)

67 g fat is 67 multiplied by 9 = 603 calories

603 divided by 2400 multiplied by 100 = 25%

At 55% carbs, 20% protein, and 25% fat, Jane's new dietary plan is in the correct range for all three macronutrients.

Monitoring your progress

Be wary of the bathroom scales. Body weight is a poor measure of the amount of fat you carry and changes measured on the scales do not necessarily reflect changes in body-fat stores.

Daily weight fluctuations are mostly due to changes in body water. You will weigh less when you are dehydrated, especially after a workout and weigh more when you are fully hydrated. Also, you will weigh several pounds less when you have low muscle glycogen stores and weigh more when you have full muscle glycogen stores (this is because carbohydrate binds to water when it is stored as glycogen). Finally, you will weigh less after emptying your bladder and bowels and weigh more if you have not emptied them for a while!

Always remember that the scales only show your weight change and do not tell you how much is due to changes in body fat, muscle mass, and body water.

So, resist the urge to step on the bathroom scales too often. Only weigh yourself once a week, first thing in the morning and on the same day of the week. In addition, take monthly body measurements of your chest, waist, hips, and buttocks with a tape measure. Measurements should be taken at the same spot each time. If measured accurately by the same person each time, these measurements provide a better indication of changes in body-fat stores and will also help you to feel encouraged if the bathroom scales are not changing.

Feeling tired, especially during practice

If you are feeling tired during practice, it is important to check that you are eating enough carbohydrates within your calorie budget so that you are training with good muscle-energy (glycogen) stores. Make sure that all your meals and snacks are based on healthy carbohydrates (whole grains, fruit, and vegetables). Enter your meals and snacks into a calorie counting app and check that you are hitting the target of 50 to 55% of your calories from carbohydrate.

Never skip on your pre- and post-training snacks – they are essential to fuel your training and help you recover for your next practice. Some people think that not having a pre-training snack, especially before an early-morning practice, will help them to burn more body fat. This isn't true, when you are training hard, your body still draws upon its preferred energy source glycogen, not your body fat. Skipping your pre-training snack will mean that you will run out of glycogen stores faster and feel tired sooner. When your glycogen stores run out, your body will begin "eating" muscles for fuel. Not being able to train as hard and having less muscle mass will reduce your daily calorie burn and make it harder for you to lose body fat.

Still struggling to lose weight?

If you are still struggling to lose weight, consider working with a registered dietitian who specializes in sports nutrition. You will receive personalized advice and a nutrition plan tailored to your training, lifestyle and food preferences.

Child athletes and weight loss

If you are a parent of a child athlete and are concerned about your child's weight, you should seek professional advice. The goal in overweight children is to slow down expected weight gain over time, or maintain their weight while they grow. This should be done under the supervision of your doctor or paediatric dietitian.

Although genetics decide your basic body type, lifestyle is more influential. In other words, the amount and type of food you eat and the activity you do each day is far more important in determining your size than your genetics.

Family involvement is essential to success. The best way to help children achieve successful changes is for the whole family to be involved. Family involvement means that all members of the family are encouraging and supporting healthier food choices. Remember, everyone in the family will benefit from the changes.

Children are very much influenced by their parents' eating patterns. As a parent, if you enjoy a range of wholesome foods, including fresh fruit and vegetables, the chances are your children will, too.

9.
IRON NEEDS OF ATHLETES

Athletes doing hard training have higher iron needs than non-athletes and can quickly deplete their iron stores. Depleted iron stores severely impair sporting performance; so, early detection of low iron stores is essential. All athletes should eat an iron rich diet to prevent iron depletion and some athletes may need to take extra iron in the form of a supplement. Let's look at the role of iron in your body and the level of iron that will ensure you are training and competing at your very best.

What your body does with iron

When you eat iron-rich foods, your body uses the iron to make new red blood cells to replace the ones that have been destroyed or lost from your body. You store extra iron as ferritin, and your body releases it when you need to make new red blood cells.

Oxygen is provided to your muscles via hemoglobin inside your red blood cells. If your iron stores (ferritin) are low, your body will not be able make enough new red blood cells and therefore you will have less oxygen going to your muscles. This will make it difficult for you to train hard and compete well.

Hard training destroys red blood cells, so you must continually replace them. Your body will also require more iron if you:

- are female with menstrual cycles;
- are going through a growth spurt;
- have a medical condition—such as celiac disease, inflammatory bowel disease, or a stomach ulcer—that reduces your body's ability to absorb iron or increases losses of iron.

A good level of Iron

There have been numerous studies on ferritin levels and athletic performance. While there are no absolutes, studies have revealed the following:

- Optimal athletic performance: ferritin 40-45ug/L
- Reduced athletic performance: ferritin less than 25μg/L

I advise athletes to maintain their ferritin level between 50 and 80μg/L to ensure a good buffer of iron stores and optimal athletic performance.

Iron in your diet

It is essential to include iron-rich foods in your diet regularly.

Animal foods such as beef, lamb, liver, pork, poultry, and fish are rich in iron and easily absorbed by your body. Beef contains the most amount of iron, so aim to eat beef about three times a week. Buy lean cuts of beef and good-quality beef burgers and meatballs. Use lean ground beef to make Bolognese, shepherd's pie, chili, lasagna, beef burgers and meatballs.

Iron-rich plant foods include baked beans, lentils, dark green vegetables (e.g., spinach, broccoli, kale), dried fruits (e.g., raisins, apricots), nuts, and iron-fortified breakfast cereals. However, iron from plant foods is not as easily absorbed by the body compared to iron from animal foods.

Eating iron-rich foods with certain other foods can significantly influence iron absorption, especially iron from plant-based foods. Foods and drinks containing vitamin C—such as oranges, tomatoes, bell peppers, kiwi fruits, and orange juice (or fruit juice fortified with vitamin C)—will help to boost your iron absorption. Alternatively, foods containing calcium such as milk, cheese, and yogurt reduce your iron absorption, as do the tannins in black or green tea, so have these foods and drinks at a different time to an iron-rich meal.

Checking your iron stores (ferritin level)

You will need to do a blood test to check your ferritin and hemoglobin levels. While hemoglobin levels are checked as part of a routine blood test, ferritin is not. You must specifically ask your doctor for the ferritin test to be included as part of your blood test.

Please note, you should avoid having your blood test done shortly after a hard practice, or when you are sick, or dehydrated, as these can cause a false reading for ferritin. If your ferritin level has dropped significantly compared to a recent blood test, it is likely due to the above reasons and the ferritin test should be repeated when you are well and having a rest day.

Once you get your test results back, ensure that your doctor gives you the ferritin number and doesn't just tell you that your ferritin is "normal." Your doctor may be using the ferritin range for the general population to make their "normal" diagnosis. For example, a female with a ferritin number of 15µg/L is considered "normal" by a medical doctor but this is very low for an athlete!

Correcting low ferritin levels

If your blood test results show that your ferritin level is below 35 µg/L, you should consider taking an iron supplement. Iron supplementation is the most effective method for increasing your iron stores quickly, especially during the competitive season. Iron supplements come in tablets or capsules and are relatively inexpensive. I recommended that you obtain your iron supplement from the pharmacy counter rather than from a health-food store. This will ensure that you receive a good dose of iron that will correct your low ferritin levels quickly. You do not need a written prescription from your doctor for iron supplements, but it is important that you inform your doctor that you are taking iron as it can interfere with the effectiveness of other medications and may cause other medical issues.

Iron is best absorbed on an empty stomach, but if you suffer from an upset stomach, take your iron supplement with some food. As with iron from food, iron supplements are better absorbed when taken with foods and drinks containing vitamin C. Also, remember that calcium-rich foods and drinks have the opposite effect and reduce iron absorption.

It is essential that you take your iron supplement several hours before or after taking other medications or any calcium or multivitamin supplement. Lastly, do not take your iron supplement within one hour of practice. Taking your iron too close to a hard practice will reduce your iron absorption and upset your stomach.

Remember, the studies show that for optimal athletic performance, you need a ferritin level of 45 µg/L. I recommend a ferritin level between 50 µg/L and 80 µg/L to ensure you have a good buffer of iron stores. It is not necessary for your ferritin level be any higher than this, as it will not further improve your performance, on the contrary, unnecessary iron may harm your health by increasing your risk of developing inflammatory conditions including cancer.

Frequency of iron tests

I recommend male athletes over the age of twelve and female athletes who are menstruating have their iron checked for hemoglobin and ferritin twice during the swim season. Ideally, this should be at the start of every season and again halfway through.

If you are taking an iron supplement, you will need to repeat your blood test every three months to ensure that your ferritin level is increasing sufficiently but not becoming too high.

Remember:

- Always eat an iron-rich diet.
- NEVER supplement with iron without having your ferritin level checked first.
- Always inform your doctor that you are supplementing with iron as it can reduce the effectiveness of other medications.
- Iron supplementation can cause constipation, nausea, and diarrhea. Taking iron with food will help to reduce these side effects.

10.
FREQUENTLY ASKED SPORTS NUTRITION QUESTIONS

This chapter answers some of the questions that I am regularly asked when I work with athletes and their families. There are many misconceptions about different foods and their benefits for athletes, so these answers should help clear up a few.

Do energy drinks help keep my energy levels up?

No.

Energy drinks are very popular, especially among teenagers. Unfortunately, the wake-up buzz from energy drinks is short-lived and followed by a prolonged period of crash and burn. The high caffeine content of energy drinks is associated with agitation, anxiety, poor sleep, rapid heart rate, and increased blood pressure. Also, some energy drinks may contain added herbal ingredients that are banned in sport.

Energy drinks should not be confused with sports drinks. Sports drinks are designed to rehydrate your body when you are training. Energy drinks do the opposite, and dehydrate your body!

Should child athletes dilute their sports drinks?

No.

There is a misconception that the sodium content in sports drinks are high; in fact, sports drinks have a similar sodium content to one serving of milk or bread. Therefore, it is not necessary for child athletes to dilute their sports drink. Secondly, diluting sports drinks have several detrimental effects:

- It reduces the amount of carbohydrates available to the muscles.
- It reduces the electrolytes available to the muscles.
- It changes the flavour, making it less desirable to drink.

Do swimmers need sports gels?

No.

Sports gels provide a highly-concentrated source of carbohydrates, and are designed for endurance athletes who must carry their fuel with them, like cyclists, distance runners, and triathletes.

Swimmers do not have to carry fuel with them and have the luxury of being able to fuel and hydrate from sports drinks placed at their end of the lane during training. At a swim meet, you have time between races to fuel up on snacks, and if you only have fifteen minutes or less before your next race, sports drinks are all that you need.

Do I need to supplement with protein powder?

No, unless you have dietary restrictions.

You can easily get all the protein you need through your usual meals and snacks. Protein powders offer no advantage over a regular diet that contains meat, fish, chicken, milk products, legumes (peas, beans and lentils), and soy products.

Supplemental protein may be useful if you have dietary restrictions; for example, if you are a vegan, have allergies to milk and soy products, or you are on a calorie restricted diet. If this sounds like you, it would be worth having your diet assessed by a registered dietitian to determine how much extra protein you need to supplement.

Can I use unsweetened almond milk instead of cow's milk to make my recovery smoothie?

Yes, with some modifications

Unfortunately, unsweetened almond milk is low in both carbohydrates and protein – two cups (500 ml) of unsweetened almond milk provides only 2 g carbohydrate and 2 g protein. On the other hand, two cups (500ml) of cow's milk provides 25g carbohydrate and 18g protein. If you are using unsweetened almond milk to make your recovery smoothie, you will need to add three servings of fruit plus half to full scoop of protein powder. This will ensure that your smoothie contains enough carbohydrate and protein to refuel and repair your muscles after training.

Do I need to take a multivitamin supplement?

Yes, recommended.

In general, if you are making healthy choices for your meals and snacks and you are consuming enough calories to maintain your body weight, a multivitamin supplement is not needed. However, I recommend that you take a daily multivitamin supplement as a health insurance to cover any potential micronutrient gaps you may have in your diet. Choose a multivitamin supplement that provides 100% of the recommended daily value for each vitamin and mineral.

A multivitamin supplement is essential if you are:

- unable to eat certain types of foods due to a food allergy or intolerance;
- vegan or eat a poorly balanced vegetarian diet;
- recovering from injury or illness;
- restricting your calorie intake;
- travelling and food choices are limited.

Be aware that you should AVOID high doses of individual vitamins and minerals unless they have been recommended by your doctor or dietitian. High doses of unnecessary vitamins and minerals can be harmful to your health.

Lastly, taking a multivitamin supplement does not give you permission to eat badly, as it will not compensate for an unhealthy junk-food diet.

Do I need to take a vitamin D supplement?

Yes, recommended.

Vitamin D has many important functions including normal growth and development of bones and maintenance of a healthy immune system. Your body makes vitamin D when you expose your skin to sunlight. It only takes about fifteen minutes of sunlight each day for your body to make enough vitamin D. Unfortunately, this is difficult in the winter months and for athletes who train and compete indoors throughout the year. In fact, one study looking at vitamin D levels in athletes revealed that vitamin D deficiency was common in swimmers who trained in an indoor pool.

It is difficult to consume enough vitamin D from food alone, as there are very few foods that are high in vitamin D. Athletes who train indoors would benefit from supplementing with 1,000 IU to 2,000 IU (25 to 50 micrograms) vitamin D daily. If you are taking a multivitamin, check the amount of vitamin D that it contains. Many multi-vitamin supplements now contain up to 1,000 IU vitamin D. Finally, make sure you take your vitamin D supplement with a meal containing some fat as your body will absorb the vitamin D better.

Vitamin D testing is not a routine blood test but you can request it from your doctor for a fee. Knowing your vitamin D level will enable you to monitor the effects of your vitamin D supplementation and check that your vitamin D blood level is in the healthy normal range.

Are there any risks associated with supplement use?

Possibly, so be careful.

Supplements are vitamins and minerals, amino acids, protein powders, mass gainers, weight-loss products, and herbal remedies. They are sometimes referred to as nutritional or dietary supplements, or natural health products.

Many supplements haven't been well studied, some can be harmful if taken in excess and can even be contaminated with ingredients that are banned in sport. Unlike the food and pharmaceutical industries, the supplement industry is subject to little government regulation.

If you are liable for drug testing under national or international programs, you should be especially cautious about supplement use. Athletes have a personal responsibility to evaluate all the risks associated with their consumption of supplements before using them, and are responsible for any prohibited substance found in their urine sample: this is known as "strict liability."

Does caffeine consumption improve swimming performance?

Possibly

Caffeine is present in many drinks, especially tea, coffee, cola drinks and energy drinks and is defined as a drug because of its effects on the body's central nervous system. Athletes, particularly endurance athletes are turning to caffeine consumption to improve their performance. Research suggests that caffeine alters the perception of fatigue in the brain, or simply put, may help athletes "go harder for longer" before fatigue sets in.

Studies demonstrated an improvement in athletic performance when 0.5 mg to 1.0 mg of caffeine per pound of body weight was consumed 30 minutes before an event. Consuming more than 1.0mg per pound body weight of caffeine did not provide further benefit. For example, if you weigh 150 pounds, this would mean consuming between 75 to 150mg caffeine, 30 minutes before your race.

However, it is important to note that individual responses to caffeine are highly varied. Some athletes found that caffeine consumption offered them no benefit at all; others found that it made their performance worse due to the negative side effects. Negative side effects include anxiety, jitters, abdominal cramps, diarrhea, and elevated heart rate. Caffeine also interferes with an athlete's ability to rest and recover and most importantly sleep well at night, resulting in fatigue and poor performance the following day.

The caffeine content in coffee varies enormously from 60 to 270 milligrams per cup! This makes it impossible to know if you are consuming too little for a performance benefit or too much for negative side-effects. Energy drinks are not recommended due to added herbal ingredients that may be banned in sport as well as their very high sugar content. The high sugar content increases the risk of an energy crash (rebound hypoglycemia) that would negatively affect your performance, especially when your race is delayed or when you are racing again later.

To avoid any guesswork, consuming pure caffeine in tablet form seems the most logical approach. Pure caffeine tablets provide an exact amount of caffeine which is quickly and easily absorbed by the body. However, the whole aspect of taking caffeine in tablet form does raise ethical issues around athletes taking a drug to gain an advantage on competitors. The American College of Sports Medicine questions *"Should the practice be condoned, as it is legal, or should it be discouraged, as it promotes the 'doping mentality' and may lead to more serious abuse?"*

Ultimately, the decision is yours. If you choose to consume caffeine before a race, it is essential that you know how your body will respond. Remember, you will respond differently to caffeine compared to another athlete. Always start off with a small amount and most importantly, do not consume caffeine for the first time before your most important race of the season! If you are taking prescription medications, you should always check with your doctor first before taking caffeine tablets. Lastly, child athletes should NOT consume caffeine as they are too susceptible to negative side effects.

I would like to have more personal nutritional advice. From whom should I seek advice?

The best source of nutritional advice is a registered dietitian. Dietitians have completed a university science degree and a post-graduate degree in nutrition and dietetics. They will provide you with evidence based nutritional advice tailored to your lifestyle and food preferences.

Look for a dietitian who specializes in sports nutrition. They will provide you with specific nutritional advice based on the demands of your sport and help you achieve any physique goals you would like to achieve.

11.
EASY RECIPES FOR HEALTHY SNACKS

Over the years, my family have tried many recipes that I have adapted to make healthier and more suitable for athletes. The following recipes have stood the test of time and are popular with my family. Best of all, they are quick and easy to make! These recipes are either gluten-free or can be made gluten-free with a slight modification.

OATY GRANOLA BARS

These make a great pre-training snack because they are high in good carbs for sustained energy and low in fat and protein for easy digestion.

This recipe makes fifteen bars and can be stored in an airtight container for many days.

Each bar provides 280 calories, 50 g carbohydrates, 7 g protein, and 6 g fat.

Ingredients

 4 cups of oats (certified gluten-free, if necessary)

 1/2 cup chopped nuts or seeds (e.g. walnuts, pecans, peanuts, pumpkin seeds)

 2 cups dried fruit (raisins, cranberries, chopped apricots; size of a pea)

 1/2 cup chocolate chips

 1 teaspoon cinnamon

 1/2 teaspoon salt

 3 large eggs

 2/3 cup honey or maple syrup

 2 teaspoons vanilla extract

Preparation

 Adjust the oven rack to the middle of the oven and set the oven to 350 F (175 C).

 Spray a 13" x 9" rimmed baking pan with oil and line the pan with parchment paper.

 In a large bowl, mix all the dry ingredients together: oats, nuts, dried fruit, chocolate chips, cinnamon, and salt.

 In another bowl, whisk together the eggs, honey, and vanilla. Add to the oatmeal mixture and stir to combine.

Transfer to the baking pan and flatten down gently with the back of a spoon.

Bake for 25 minutes until edges turn golden brown.

Let it cool completely before slicing into fifteen bars.

POWER FRUIT LOAF

I adapted this recipe from a basic fruit loaf recipe that I was given in New Zealand. I reduced the amount of added sugar and increased the amount of dried fruit. I also added chia seeds for extra "good fats."

This fruit loaf makes a great pre-training snack and can be eaten cold or toasted with butter. The loaf can be sliced into twelve servings.

One serving provides 300 calories, 60 g carbs, 7 g protein, and 3 g fat.

Ingredients

1 cup oats (certified gluten-free, if necessary)

1/3 cup chia seeds

2 cups dried fruit (for example, raisins, cranberries, chopped apricots)

1 cup brown sugar

2 ½ cups of reduced fat milk (2% or less)

2 cups whole-wheat flour (or gluten-free all-purpose baking flour)

1 teaspoon baking powder

Preparation

Preheat your oven to 300 F (150 C). Lightly oil a large loaf pan.

Soak the oats, chia seeds, dried fruit, and sugar in the milk for ten minutes. Stir in the flour and baking powder. If you use gluten free all purpose flour, you will need to add more milk (try three cups instead of two). The mixture should be thick. Spoon the mixture into the loaf pan and bake for 90 minutes. Cool on a wire rack before slicing.

BERRY BANANA MUFFINS

Most shop-bought and traditional muffin recipes are high in fat, sugar and calories. The fat in this recipe has been reduced by substituting some of the oil with non-fat plain Greek yogurt. The sweetness in these muffins is provided by the ripe bananas and a small amount of honey.

This recipe makes twelve muffins.

Each muffin provides 220 calories, 35 g carbohydrates, 6 g protein, 7 g fat.

Ingredients

  3 medium bananas, well mashed

  3/4 cup non-fat plain Greek yogurt

  1/2 cup honey

  1/3 cup healthy oil (e.g. olive or canola oil)

  1 teaspoon of vanilla extract

  2 cups of whole-wheat flour (or gluten-free all-purpose baking flour)

  2 teaspoons baking powder

  1/2 teaspoon baking soda

  1/2 teaspoon salt

  1 generous cup of frozen blueberries

Preparation

Place a wire rack in the centre of the oven, then preheat to 425 F (220 C). Lightly spray a twelve-cup muffin pan with olive oil or line with baking cups.

In a large bowl, place the bananas, yogurt, honey, oil, and vanilla. Stir together until well mixed. In a separate bowl, mix together the flour, baking powder, baking soda, and salt. Add the dry ingredients to the banana mixture and stir until just combined. Fold in the frozen blueberries gently, being careful not to over-mix.

Spoon the batter into the prepared muffin pan. Place the muffin pan in the oven and reduce the heat to 400 F (205 C). Bake for 20 to 25 minutes, or until the tops spring back when lightly touched. Leave the muffins in the pan for 10 to 15 minutes before transferring to a cooling rack.

Let the muffins cool completely before storing them in an airtight container for up to three days. Alternatively, you can store them in the freezer and you will always have a healthy snack on hand. I put a frozen muffin in my son's lunchbox before he leaves for school and the muffin has defrosted by morning break.

HEALTHY TRAIL MIX

Homemade trail mix only takes a few minutes and you can create your own using your favourite ingredients.

Make your own trail mix by mixing ingredients in these proportions. Trail mix is moderately high in fat so allow at least one hour to digest before training.

Ingredients

3 cups of dried fruit	Choose from apples, tart cherries, cranberries, blueberries, apricots, raisins, and banana chips. My favourite combination is 2 cups of raisins plus ½ cup each of tart cherries and apricots.
2 cups of nuts	Choose from almonds, pistachios, cashews, peanuts and walnuts. My favourite combination is ⅔ cup each of almonds, pistachios and cashews.
1/2 cup of seeds	Choose from sunflower, pumpkin, and hemp seeds. My favourite seeds are pumpkin.

2 cups of whole-grain, low sugar breakfast cereal

1 cup of dark chocolate chips

Preparation

Combine the nuts, dried fruit, seeds, cereal and chocolate chips in these proportions and store in an airtight container. Shake well before scooping out into sixteen ½-cup or twelve ¾-cup servings.

A ½ cup serving provides 225 calories, 30 g carbohydrates, 6 g protein, 10 g fat

A ¾ cup serving provides 300 calories, 40 g carbohydrates, 7 g protein, 13 g fat

SMOOTHIES

Smoothies make an easy breakfast on the run and excellent pre-training and recovery snacks. They're easy to drink, taste great and are good for your health.

Smoothies can be made from all kinds of soft fruits: bananas, strawberries, blueberries, raspberries, and peaches, etc. You can even add some leafy greens such as spinach or kale for added nutrition (apart from the give-away green colour, you won't know they're in the smoothie). Blend the fruit and greens with combinations of milk, yogurt, and juice. Have fun experimenting and come up with your own signature smoothie.

The following smoothie recipes are popular with my family:

<u>Blueberry Smoothie</u>: 1 cup blueberries, 1 large banana, large handful of greens, 2 cups of low-fat milk (2% or less)

This provides 445 calories, 70 g carbohydrates, 20 g protein, 10g fat

<u>Mango Smoothie</u>: 1 cup mango chunks, 1 large banana, 2 cups of low-fat milk (2% or less)

This provides 465 calories, 75 g carbohydrates, 20 g protein, 10g fat

<u>Strawberry Yogurt Smoothie</u>: 1 cup strawberries, 1 cup low-fat vanilla yogurt, 1 cup of low-fat milk (2% or less)

This provides 370 calories, 65 g carbohydrates, 17 g protein, 8g fat

Peanut Butter Smoothie: 1 large banana, 1 tablespoon of peanut butter, 1 cup low- fat milk, 1 cup low-fat vanilla yogurt, 1 tablespoon of honey

This provides 560 calories, 85 g carbohydrates, 24 g protein, 16g fat

The peanut butter smoothie is high in calories and is a good choice if you are trying to gain weight. As this smoothie is higher in fat, allow at least one hour to digest before training.

FRENCH TOAST

My sons enjoy making this recipe. It makes a great recovery breakfast after a morning practice.

Two slices of French toast with ½ banana (sliced) and one tablespoon of maple syrup provides 330 calories, 55 g carbohydrates 13 g protein, and 8 g of fat.

Four slices of French toast with 1 banana (sliced) and two tablespoons of maple syrup provides 660 calories, 110 g carbohydrates 26 g protein, and 16 g of fat.

The following recipe makes four slices of French toast:

Ingredients

    2 eggs

    1/4 cup milk

    1/4 teaspoon vanilla extract

    1/4 teaspoon ground cinnamon

    4 slices of 100% whole-grain bread

Preparation

    In a bowl, beat the eggs with a whisk until foamy, then whisk in the milk, vanilla, and cinnamon.

    Heat a lightly oiled frying pan over a medium to low heat.

Dip the slices of bread into the egg mixture, turning to coat them thoroughly. Let any excess drip back into the bowl.

Place the coated bread slices into the hot pan. Cook until both sides are nicely browned—about two minutes for each side.

WHOLE-WHEAT PANCAKES WITH FRUIT

This pancake recipe makes a great recovery breakfast when served with plenty of fruits, lean bacon, and maple syrup. My sons devour these pancakes after a gruelling three hour Saturday morning practice.

One pancake with ½ banana and ½ cup strawberries, two slices of back bacon, and one tablespoon of maple syrup provides 360 calories, 75 g carbohydrates, 14 g protein, and 5 g of fat.

The basic recipe makes six thick pancakes.

Ingredients

2 cups whole-wheat flour (or gluten-free all-purpose baking flour)

2 tsp baking powder

2 eggs (beaten)

1 teaspoon of vanilla extract (optional)

2 cups milk

Preparation

Place the flour and baking powder into a large bowl and stir with a fork. In a small bowl, beat the egg until it is frothy, then add the milk (and vanilla extract). Make a well in the middle of the flour mixture and add the egg and milk, then combine the mixture. It will look a little lumpy, but that's OK. The lumps will disappear during cooking and it is best not to over-mix. Add more milk if you prefer a thinner consistency.

Heat a lightly oiled frying pan over a medium heat. Pour or scoop the pancake mixture into the pan and brown the pancake on both sides. Wait until lots of bubbles form on the surface of the pancake before turning.

RESOURCES

Here are some of the sports nutrition research papers that were used when writing this book. I have also included some good sports nutrition textbooks and websites for your information.

Chapter 2: Nutrition Before Training

Sherman WM, Costill DL, Fink WJ, Miller JM. Effect of exercise-diet manipulation on muscle glycogen and its subsequent utilization during performance. *Int J Sports Med* 1981; 2: 114-118

Saltin B, Gollnick PD. Fuel for muscular exercise: role of carbohydrate. In: Horton ES, Terjung RL, eds. *Exercise, Nutrition, and Energy Metabolism.* New York: Macmillan; 1988: 45-53

Walker JL, Heigenhauser GJ, Hultman E, Spriet LL. Dietary carbohydrate, muscle glycogen content, and endurance performance in well trained women. *J Appl Physiol* 2000; 88: 2151-2158

Coyle EF, Coggan AR, Hemmert MK, Lowe RC, Walters TJ. Substrate usage during prolonged exercise following a pre-exercise meal. *J Appl Physiol* 1985; 59: 429-433

Marmy-Conus N, Fabris S, Proietto J, Hargreaves M. Preexercise glucose ingestion and glucose kinetics during exercise. *J Appl Physiol* 1996; 81: 853-857

Hargreaves M, Costill DL, Fink WJ, King DS, Fielding RA. Effect of pre-exercise carbohydrate feedings on endurance cycling performance. *Med Sci Sports Exerc* 1987; 19: 33-36

Goodpaster BH, Costill DL, Fink WJ, et al. The effects of pre-exercise starch ingestion on endurance performance. *Int J Sports Med* 1996; 17: 366-372

Chryssanthopoulos C, Williams C, Wilson W, Asher, L, Hearne L. Comparison between carbohydrate feedings before and during exercise on running performance during a 30-km treadmill time trial. *Int J Sport Nutr* 1994; 374-386

Hargreaves M, Finn JP, Withers RT, Halbert JA, Scroop GC, Mackay M, Snow RJ, Carey MF. Effect on muscle glycogen availability on maximal exercise performance. *Eur J Appl Physiol* 1997; 75: 188-192

Chapter 3: Fluids and Fuel During Training

Costill DL. Gastric emptying of fluids during exercise. In: Gisolfi CV, Lamb DR, eds. *Fluid Homeostasis During Exercise (Perspectives in Exercise Science and Sports Medicine).* Vol 3. Indianapolis: Benchmark Press; 1990: 97-121

Coyle EF. Fluid and fuel intake during exercise. *J Sport Sci* 2004; 22: 39-55

Yaspelkis BB, Patterson JG, Anderla PA, Ding Z, Ivy JL. Carbohydrate supplementation spares muscle glycogen during variable-intensity exercise. *J Appl Physiol* 1993; 75: 1477-1485

Hargreaves M, Costill DL, Coggan AR, Fink WJ, Nishibata I. Effect of carbohydrate feedings on muscle glycogen utilization and exercise performance. *Med Sci Sports Exerc* 1984; 16: 219-222

Below P, Mora-Rodriguez R, Gonzalez-Alonso J, Coyle EF. Fluid and carbohydrate ingestion independently improve performance during 1h of intense exercise. *Med Sci Sports Exerc* 1995; 27: 200-210

Jenkendrup AE. Carbohydrate intake during exercise and performance. *Nutrition* 2004; 20: 669-677

American College of Sports Medicine. Position Stand on exercise and fluid replacement. *Med Sci Sports Exerc* 1996, 28: i-vii

National Athletic Training Association. Fluid replacement for athletes. *J Ath Train* 2000; 35: 212-224

Cox GR, et al. Body mass changes and voluntary fluid changes of elite level water polo players and swimmers. *J. Sci & Med*, 2002,183-193

Chapter 4: Nutrition After Training

Kerksick C, et al. (2008). Nutrient timing. *Journal of the International Society of Sports Nutrition*, 5: 17-29

Coyle EF, Coyle EL. Carbohydrates that speed recovery from training. *Phys. Sports med.*, 1993; 21: 1 11

Shinkai S, Watanabe S, Asai H, Shek PN. Cortisol response to exercise and post-exercise suppression of blood lymphocyte subset counts. *Int J Sports Med* 1996; 17: 597-603

Koeslag JH. Post-exercise ketosis and the hormone response to exercise: a review. *Med Sci Sports Exerc* 1982; 4: 327

Nieman DC. Nutrition, exercise, and immune system function. In: Wheeler KB, Lombardo JA, eds. *Clinics in Sports Medicine: Nutritional Aspects of Exercise*. Vol 18. Philadelphia: WB Saunders; 1999: 537-538

Costill DL, Sherman WM, Fink WJ, Maresh C, Witten M, Miller J. The role of dietary carbohydrate in muscle glycogen resynthesis after strenuous running. *Am J Clin Nutr* 1981; 34: 1831-1836

Ivy JL, Katz AL, Cutler CL, Sherman WM, Coyle EF. Muscle glycogen synthesis after exercise: effect of time of carbohydrate ingestion. *J Appl Physiol* 1988; 64: 1480-1485

Ivy JL, Golforth HW, Damon BD, McCauley TR, Parsons EC, Price TB. Early post-exercise muscle glycogen recovery is enhanced with a carbohydrate-protein supplement. *J Appl Physiol* 2002; 93: 1337-1344

Carrithers JA, Williamson DL, Gallagher PM, Godard MP, Schulze KE, Trappe SW. Effects of postexercise carbohydrate-protein feedings on muscle glycogen restoration. *J Appl Physiol* 2000; 88: 1976-1982

Levenhagen DK, Gresham JD, Carlson MG, Maron DL, Borel MJ, Flakoll PJ. Post-exercise nutrient intake timing in humans is critical to recovery of leg glucose and protein homeostasis. *Am J Physiol* 2001; 280: E982-E993

Romano BC, Todd MK, Saunders MJ. Effect of 4:1 ratio carbohydrate/protein beverage on endurance performance, muscle damage and recovery. *Med Sci Sports* Exerc 2004; 36(5): S126

Symons T et al. A moderate serving of high-quality protein maximally stimulates skeletal muscle protein synthesis in young and elderly subjects. *Journal of the American Dietetic Association* 2009; 109: 1582-1586

Chapter 5: Everyday Meals and Snacks for Athletes

Lambert EV, Goedecke JH. The role of dietary macronutrients in optimizing endurance performance. *Curr Sport Med Rep* 2003; 2(4): 194-201

Tarnopolsky M. Protein requirements for endurance athletes. *Nutrition* 2004; 20: 662-668

American College of Sports Medicine, American Dietetic Association, Dietitians of Canada. Joint position stand on nutrition and athletic performance. *J Am Diet Assoc* 2009; 109(3):509-527

Harvard Health Publications. The Good, The Bad and the in-between. Feb 2015

Chapter 6: Competition Nutrition

Bangsbo J, Nooregaard L, Thorsoe F. The effect of carbohydrate diet on intermittent exercise performance. *Int J Sports Med* 1992; 13: 152-7

Bergstrom J, Hermansen L, Hultman E, Saltin B. Diet, muscle glycogen and physical performance. *Acta Physiol Scand* 1967; 71: 140-50

Coyle EF: Timing and method of increased carbohydrate intake to cope with heavy training, competition and recovery. *J Sports Sci.* 1991; 9 (suppl): 29-52

Noakes TD, Rehrer NJ, Maughan RJ. The importance of volume in regulating gastric emptying. *Med Sci Sports Exerc* 1991; 23: 307-13

Rehrer NJ, Van Kemenade M, Meester W, Brouns F, Saris WHM. Gastrointestinal complaints in relation to dietary intake in triathletes. *Int J Sport Nutr* 1992; 2: 48-59

Chapter 7: Gaining Weight and Muscle Mass

Meredith CN, Zachin MJ, Frontera WR, Evans WJ. Dietary protein requirements and body protein metabolism in endurance trained men. *J Appl Physiol* 1989; 66: 2850-6

Roy BD, Fowles JR, Hill R, Tarnopolsky MA. Macronutrient intake and whole body protein metabolism following resistance exercise. Med Sci Sports Exerc, Aug 2000

Wlalberg-Rankin J. Changing body weight and composition in athletes. Carmel, IN: Cooper Publishing Group, 1998

Dietary Reference Intakes for Energy, Carbohydrate, Fiber, Fat, Fatty Acids, Cholesterol, Protein, and Amino Acids, Institute of Medicine of the National Academies, 2002 and 2005, the National Academies Press, N.W. Washington, DC 20001

Brooks GA, Butte NF, Rand WM, Flatt JP, Caballero B. Chronicle of the Institute of Medicine physical activity recommendation came to be among dietary recommendations. *Am J Clin Nutr.* 2004;79(5):921S-930

Chapter 8: Losing Body Fat

Bilsborough SA, Crowe TC. Low carbohydrate diets: what are the potential short term and long term health implications? *Asia Pacific J Clin Nutr* 200312(4): 396-404

O'Connor H, Sullivan T, Caterson I. Weight loss and the athlete, in Clinical Sports Nutrition, 2nd edition, eds L.Burke, V.Deakin, chapter 7 (McGraw-Hill Book Company, Sydney, 2000), pp 146-176

Almeras N, Lemieux S, Bouchard C, Tremblay A. Fat gain in female swimmers. *Physiolog Behav* 1997; 61: 811-17

Donnelly JE, Jakicic J, Gunderson S. Diet and body composition: effect of very low calorie diets and exercise. *Sports Med* 1991; 12: 237-49

Stager JM, Cordain L. Relationship of body composition to swimming performance in female swimmers. *J Swim Res.* 1984; 1: 21-4

Flynn ML, Costill DL, Kirwa JP, Mitchell JB., Houmard JA, Fink WJ, Beltz JD, D'Acquisto LJ. Fat storage in athletes: metabolic and hormonal responses to swimming and running. *International Journal of Sports Medicine 1990*, 11, 433-440

Jang KT, Flynn MG, Costill DL, Kirwan JP, Houmard JA, Mitchell JB, D'Acquisto LJ. Energy balance in competitive swimmers and runners. *Journal of Swimming Research* 1987, 3, 19-23

Bellisle F, Drewnowski A. Intense sweeteners, energy intake and the control of body weight. *Eur J Clin Nutr* 2007; 61: 691-700

Frank GK, Oberndorfer TA, Simmons AN, et al. Sucrose activates human taste pathways differently from artificial sweetener. *Neuroimage_2008*; 39: 1559-69

Dietary Reference Intakes for Energy, Carbohydrate, Fiber, Fat, Fatty Acids, Cholesterol, Protein, and Amino Acids, Institute of Medicine of the National Academies, 2002 and 2005, the National Academies Press, N.W. Washington, DC 20001

Brooks GA, Butte NF, Rand WM, Flatt JP, Caballero B. Chronicle of the Institute of Medicine physical activity recommendation came to be among dietary recommendations. Am J Clin Nutr 2004;79(5):921S-930

Chapter 9: Iron Needs of Athletes

Akabas SR, Dolins KR. Micronutrient requirements of physically active women: What can we learn from iron? *The American Journal of Clinical Nutrition* 2005, 81(Suppl.), 1246S-1251S.

Auersperger I, Knap B, Jerin A, Blagus R, Lainscak M, Skitek M, Skof B. Effects of 8 weeks of endurance running on hepcidin concentrations, inflammatory parameters, and iron status in female runners. *International Journal of Sport Nutrition and Exercise Metabolism* 2012, 22, 55-63

Chatard J, Mujika I, Guy C, Lacour, J. Anaemia and iron deficiency in athletes: Practical recommendations for treatment. *Journal of Sports Medicine* 1999, 27(4), 229-240

Cowell BS, Rosenbloom CA, Skinner R, Summers SH. Policies on screening female athletes for iron deficiency in NCAA Division-IA institutions. *International Journal of Sport Nutrition and Exercise Metabolism* 2003, 13, 277- 28

Fallon, KE. Screening for haematological and iron- related abnormalities in elite athletes-analysis of 576 cases. *Journal of Science and Medicine in Sport* 2008,11, 329-336

Koehler K, Braun H, Achtzehn S, Hildebrand U, Predel H, Mester J, Schanzer W. Iron status in elite young athletes: gender-dependent influences of diet and exercise. *European Journal of Applied Physiology* 2011, 112, 513-523

Milic R, Martinovic J, Dopsaj M, Dopsaj V. (2011). Haematological and iron-related parameters in male and female athletes according to different metabolic energy demands. *European Journal of Applied Physiology* 2011, 111, 449- 458.

Nielsen, P. & Nachtigall, D. Iron supplementation in athletes: Current recommendations. *Journal of Sports Medicine* 1998, 26(4), 207-216

Papanikolaou, G. & Pantopoulos, K. Iron metabolism and toxicity. *Toxicology and Applied Pharmacology* 2004, 202(2), 199-211

Ryan, M. Preventing and treating iron deficiency in athletes. *Athletic Therapy Today* 2004, 9(2), 56-57

Suedekum NA, Dimeff RJ: Iron and the athlete. *Curr Sports Med Rep* 2005, 4: 1 99-202

Friedmann B, Weller E, Mairbaurl H, Bartsch P. Effects of iron repletion on red blood cell volume and exercise performance. *Med Sci Sports Exerc* 2000, 32: S75

Klingshirn LA, Pate RR, Bourque SP, Davis JM, Sargent RG. Effect of iron supplementation on endurance capacity in iron-depleted female runners. *Med Sci Sports Exerc* 1992, 24:819-824

Tsalis G, Nikolaidis MG, Mougios V. Effects of iron intake through food or supplement on iron status and performance of healthy adolescent swimmers during a training season. *Int J Sports Med* 2004, 25: 306-313

Chapter 10: Frequently Asked Questions

CAFFEINE

Yelverton, J. Caffeine Improves Sprint-Distance Performance among Division II Collegiate Swimmers. **The Sports Journal** 2014

Hogervorst E, Bandelow S, Schmitt J, Jentjens R, Oliveira M, Allgrove J, Gleeson M. Caffeine improves physical and cognitive performance during exhaustive exercise. *Medicine and Science in Sports and Exercise* 2008, 40(10), 1841-1851

Astorino TA, Roberson DW. Efficacy of acute caffeine ingestion for short-term high-intensity exercise performance. *Journal of Strength and Conditioning Research*/National Strength & Conditioning Association 2010, 24(1), 257-265

Collomp K, Ahmaidi S, Chatard JC, Audran M, Prefaut C. Benefits of caffeine ingestion on sprint performance in trained and untrained swimmers. *European Journal of Applied Physiology* 1992, 64, 377-380

Sökmen B, Armstrong LE, Kraemer WJ, Casa DJ, Dias JC, Judelson DA, Maresh CM. Caffeine use in sports: considerations for the athlete. *Journal of Strength and Conditioning Research* 2008, 22(3), 978-986

VITAMIN D

Constantini NW, Arieli R, Chodick G, Dubnov-Raz G. High prevalence of vitamin D insufficiency in athletes and dancers. *Clin J Sport Med* 2010, 20, 368–371

Halliday TM, Peterson NJ, Thomas JJ, Kleppinger K, Hollis BW, Larson-Meyer DE. Vitamin D status relative to diet, lifestyle, injury, and illness in college athletes. *Med Sci Sports & Exercise* 2011, 43,335–343

Moran D., McClung J., Kohen T. & Lieberman H. Vitamin D and physical performance. *Sports Medicine* 2013, 43: 601-611

Lewis RM, Redzic M, Thomas DT. The effects of season-long vitamin D supplementation on collegiate swimmers and divers. *International Journal of Sport Nutrition and Exercise Metabolism* 2013, 23, 431–440

FURTHER READING

Antonio J, Kalman D, Stout JR, Greenwood M, Willoughby DS, Haff GG. *Essentials of Sports Nutrition and Supplements.* Humana Press, 2008

Benardot D. *Advanced Sports Nutrition.* Human Kinetics; 2006

Burke L, Deakin V. *Clinical Sports Nutrition.* Sydney: McGraw-Hill; 2005

Clark N. *Sports Nutrition Guidebook.* Human Kinetics; 2008

Taub-Dix B. *Read it Before You Eat it.* Plume; 2010

IOC Nutrition Working Group. *Nutrition for Athletes;* 2012

Useful sports nutrition websites

Dietitians of Canada: www.dietitians.ca

Coaches Association of Canada (CAC): www.coach.ca

Sports Dietitians UK: www.sportsdietitians.org.uk

Sports Dietitians Australia: www.sportsdietitians.com.au

ACKNOWLEDGEMENTS

I would like to thank my husband Alasdair for his love, patience and advice. He spent many hours reading through earlier drafts of this book and gave me invaluable feedback. Thank you also to my three sons, Robert, Finlay, and Rory. They have enabled me to make my advice realistic and practical for every busy parent. Also, huge thanks to my twin sister Emma and my mum Elsa for their love and support and for encouraging me all the way. Lastly, I would like to thank Head Coach Todd Melton as well as the parents and swimmers of the Foothills Stingrays swim club for giving me the inspiration to write this book. Their enthusiasm and support has been wonderful!